Manifesto
for
Islamic Reform

Edip Yuksel

BrainbowPress
Iconoclastic Books

www.19.org
www.yuksel.org
www.islamicreform.org
www.brainbowpress.com

ISBN: 978-0-9796715-6-2

9 780979 671562

50995

ISBN 978-0-9796715-6-2

Printed in the United States of America

10 9 8 7 6 5 4 3

2

CONTENTS

4

Manifesto For Islamic Reform[1]

> "O people, a proof has come to you from
> your Lord, and We have sent down to you a
> guiding light." (4:174)
>
> "...and do not make corruption on the Earth
> after it has been reformed..." (7:85)
>
> "It is one of the great ones. A warning to
> humanity. For any among you who wishes
> to progress or regress." (74:36-37)

The influence of the religion concocted by clerics during the Umayyad and Abbasid dynasties is still dominant in Muslim countries. The idea that the Quran is incomplete, unintelligible, and insufficient for spiritual guidance created a huge demand for religious books, and the scholars and clergymen supplied volumes of them. The masses were told that those books were going to complete, explain, and detail the Quranic revelation. These clerics thus implied that God was not a wise and articulate author; He could not make His message sufficiently clear and He failed to provide guidance on many issues, even issues involving important spiritual principles and practices. Without these supplementary books, the Quran was of limited use to the individual seeking religious guidance. Some even went so far as to declare that reading the Quran alone would mislead the reader. Numerous books of *hadith* and sectarian jurisprudence (*sharia*) were labeled "authentic" and for all practical purposes, replaced the Quran. The Quran was not a book to be understood on its own; people needed to read books written by professional narrators, collectors, editors, and scholars of hearsay and speculation. Many people got lost among the volumes of books written to interpret and explain the Quran and did not find sufficient time to study the Quran itself. The privileged few who did find that time had little chance of understanding it, since their minds were tainted with man-made religious instructions, and their logic had been corrupted by contradictory teachings or what we might call "holy viruses."

Although religious scholars, clerics and their blind followers have always demonstrated the utmost formal respect for the Quran as physical media (the leather or paper on which the verses of the Quran were written), they lost faith in, and respect for its message. Verses of the Quran are hung in high places on the walls, touched and treated with utmost reverence, yet the so-called Muslims rarely refer to them for their guidance. They are too confused by the

---

[1] First published in 2007, as the appendix of the Quran: a Reformist Translation.

contradictory and tangled maze of thousands of *hadith* falsely attributed to Muhammad and lost among the trivial details of sectarian books. When they occasionally refer to the Quran, it is most likely to be in an abusive manner, abusing the verses by taking them out of context and using them as slogans to declare holy wars or to justify aggression. The Quran that liberated people from the darkness of ignorance was transformed, soon after Muhammad's departure, to a book whose verses were recited for the dead, an amulet carried by the mentally and physically sick, and a paper idol to be revered and feared.

Though the Quran is considered one of the most read books, millions of the followers of Sunni and Shiite sects read the Quran without understanding it. Even if their native language is Arabic, they are taught not to trust their understanding. The Quran might be the most read book, but unfortunately, due to the concerted effort of religious clerics, it has been turned into the least understood and the least appreciated popular book in history.

When the mass reversion from the progressive and enlightening message of the Quran started, those who rejected the fabricated *hadith* and *sunna*, the Arab version of the Jewish Mishna and Gemara, were labeled "*murtad*" (apostates) and were threatened, tortured and murdered by the followers of *hadith* and *sunna*. For instance, a critical study of the Muslim history will reveal that Abu Hanifa was one of those courageous monotheists (*hanif*) who was persecuted during both the Umayyad and Abbasid dynasties. During his lifetime, he was accused of not accepting *hadith*. However, the murderers took advantage of his growing reputation after his death and led the creation of a Sunni sect falsely attributed to him.

The Origins of Sectarian Teachings

After the death of the prophet Muhammad, a diabolic event happened. In direct contradiction to the teachings of the Quran, male clerics dedicated the religion not to God alone, but to a "holy" corporation consisting of:

- God +
- Muhammad +
- Muhammad's companions +
- The companions of Muhammad's companions +
- Early sect leaders +
- Late sect leaders +
- Early scholars of a particular sect +
- Late scholars of a particular sect, and so on.

The product of this corporation was the *hadith* (teachings attributed to Muhammad), the *sunna* (actions attributed to Muhammad), the *ijma* (consensus of a select group of early scholars), and the *sharia* (religious decrees by early scholars). The result was numerous hostile factions that afflicted a great amount of division and atrocities in the land about thirty years after the departure of

6

Muhammad (6:159; 23:52-56). This concoction of medieval Arab/Christian/Jewish cultures was introduced to the masses as God's infallible religion, as delivered by the last prophet. The only thing actually delivered by God to Muhammad, however, was the text of the Holy Quran, which is set out as the final and authoritative divine message to humankind:

> 75:18-19 Once We recite it, you shall follow such a recitation (Quran). Then, it is We who will explain it.

Unfortunately, ignorance, intolerance, misogynist teachings, superstitions, and outdated practices have accumulated over the centuries in interpreting and translating the holy book of Islam. It is time to re-introduce the actual message of the Quran. It is time to remove the accumulated layers of man-made dogmas and traditions that have attached themselves to the text (6:21; 7:29; 9:31; 16:52; 39:2,11,14; 40:14,65; 42:21; 45.17; 74:1-56; 98:5).

Under a very cruel theocratic state terror, many men mobilized to participate in the creation that we rightly call Hislam. They did not have much chance to add or subtract to what was considered The Quran, but there was a lot of room for innovations, superstitions, additions and distortions through fabricating *hadith*. When a man from Bukhara started collecting hearsay more than two hundred years after the departure of the prophet Muhammad, the landscape and social demographics were fertile for all kinds of theological concoctions and mutations. Those people and their parents had participated in numerous sectarian wars and atrocities. Many educated Gentiles, Christians and Jews were converted to Islam for dubious reasons. Most of these converts had never experienced a paradigm change; they just found it convenient to integrate their culture and most of their previous religious ideas with the new one. To justify and promote their version of religion, the elite started packaging and introducing their religious, cultural, and political ideas and practices under the brand names of *hadith*, *sunna*, commentaries, and *fatwas*. Additionally, they fabricated numerous stories called "*asbab ul-nuzul*" (the reasons for revelation) about why each verse was revealed, thereby distorting the meaning or limiting the scope of many Quranic verses. There was a great effort and competition to distort the meaning of words, taking them out of context to promote the agenda of a certain religion, culture, tribe, sect, cult, or king. Male chauvinists, hermits, misogynists too took advantage of this deformation movement. Hearsay statements attributing words and deeds to Muhammad and his idolized comrades became the most powerful tool or Trojan horse, for the promotion of diverse political propaganda, cultural assimilation, and even commercial advertisement. As a result, the Quran was deserted and its message was heavily distorted.[2]

---

[2] There are hundreds of books written on this subject. Mahmud Abu Rayya's book, *Adwa' 'ala al-Sunna al-Muhammadiya*, is an outstanding book since Abu Rayya was a contemporary Sunni scholar and he used the so-called "authentic" sources to demonstrate the manifold problems inflicting *hadith* and *sunna*. It can be considered

Soon after Muhammad's death, thousands of *hadith*s (words attributed to Muhammad) were fabricated and two centuries later collected, and centuries later compiled and written in the so-called "authentic" *hadith* books:

- to support the teaching of a particular sect against another (such as, what nullifies ablution; which sea food is prohibited);
- to flatter or justify the authority and practice of a particular king against dissidents (such as, *Mahdy* and *Dajjal*);
- to promote the interest of a particular tribe or family (such as, favoring the Quraysh tribe or Muhammad's family);
- to justify sexual abuse and misogyny (such as, Aisha's age; barring women from leading *Sala* prayers);
- to justify violence, oppression and tyranny (such as, torturing members of *Urayna* and *Uqayla* tribes; massacring the Jewish population in Medina; assassinating a female poet for her critical poems);
- to exhort more rituals and righteousness (such as, *nawafil* prayers);
- to validate superstitions (such as, magic; worshiping the black stone near the *Kaba*);
- to prohibit certain things and actions (such as, prohibiting drawing animal and human figures; playing musical instruments; chess);
- to import Jewish and Christian beliefs and practices (such as, death by stoning; circumcision; head scarf; hermitism; rosary);
- to resurrect pre-Islamic beliefs and practices common among Meccans (such as, intercession; slavery; tribalism; misogyny);
- to please crowds with stories (such as the story of *Miraj* (ascension to heaven) and bargaining for prayers);
- to idolize Muhammad and claim his superiority to other messengers (such as, numerous miracles, including splitting the moon);
- to defend *hadith* fabrications against monotheists (such as, condemning those who find the Quran alone sufficient); and even
- to advertise products of a particular farm (such as, the benefits of dates grown in a town called *Ajwa*).

---

an honest confession of a Sunni scholar regarding the amount of dirt that seeped into the so-called "authentic *hadith* books." We highly recommend Rashad Khalifa's groundbreaking book, *Quran, Hadith and Islam*. This book breaks the spell of diabolic teachings by reminding us of the relevant Quranic verses; results show that it provides one of the fastest detoxification programs. Ahmad Kassim's *Hadith: a Reevaluation* is another good book. My book, *19 Questions For Muslim Scholars*, though originally a thin book, contains nineteen selected critical analyses and discussions on selected issues. A recent book by Dr. Caner Taslaman, *Fabricated Religion versus Quranic Religion*, is noteworthy for its comprehensive evaluation of sectarian teachings and the powerful arguments against them. For the Jewish influence on Sunni or Shiite versions of Muhammadanism, I recommend a Turkish book, *Tefsirde Israiliyat* (Jewish Stories in Commentaries of the Quran) by Abdullah Aymaz.

In addition to the above mentioned reasons, many *hadith* were fabricated to explain the meaning of the "difficult" Quranic words or phrases, or to distort the meaning of verses that contradicted the fabricated *hadith*, or to provide trivial information not mentioned in the Quran (such as, Saqar, 2:187; 8:35...).

Islam versus Sunni and Shiite Religions

Let's first check the Quran and enumerate some of the characteristics of Islam, the system of peace, submission and surrender to God alone.

Islam

- is not a proper name, but a descriptive noun coming from the Arabic root of surrendering/submission/peace, used by God to describe the system delivered by all His messengers and prophets (5:111; 10:72; 98:5), which reached another stage with Abraham (4:125; 22:78).
- is peacefully surrendering to God alone (2:112,131; 4:125; 6:71; 22:34; 40:66).
- is a system with universal principles, which are in harmony with nature (3:83; 33:30; 35:43).
- requires objective evidence besides personal experience (3:86; 2:111; 21:24; 74:30).
- demands conviction not based on wishful thinking or feelings, but based on reason and evidence (17:36; 4:174; 8:42; 10:100; 11:17; 74:30-31).
- esteems knowledge, education, and learning (35:28; 4:162; 9:122; 22:54; 27:40; 29:44,49).
- promotes scientific inquiry regarding the evolution of humankind on earth (29:20).
- rejects clergymen and intermediaries between God and people (2:48; 9:31-34).
- condemns profiteering from religion (9:34; 2:41,79,174; 5:44; 9:9).
- stands for liberty, accountability, and defiance of false authorities (6:164).
- stands for freedom of expression (2:256; 18:29; 10:99; 88:21-22).
- requires consultation and representation in public affairs (42:38; 5:12).
- promotes a democratic system where participation of all citizens is encouraged and facilitated (58:11).
- prohibits bribery, and requires strict rules against the influence of interest groups and corporations in government (2:188).
- requires election of officials based on qualifications and principles of justice (4:58).
- promises justice for everyone, regardless of their creed or ethnicity (5:8).
- acknowledges the rights of citizens to publicly petition against injustices committed by individuals or government (4:148).

- encourages the distribution of wealth, economic freedom and social welfare (2:215, 59:7).
- promotes utmost respect to individuals (5:32).
- relates the quality of a society to the quality of individuals comprising it (13:11).
- recognizes and protects individual right's to privacy (49:12).
- recognizes the right to the presumption of innocence and right to confront the accuser (49:12).
- provides protection for witnesses (2:282).
- does not hold innocent people responsible for the crimes of others (53:38).
- protects the right to personal property (2:85,188; 4:29; exception 24:29; 59:6-7).
- discourages a non-productive economy (2:275; 5:90; 3:130).
- encourages charity and caring for the poor (6:141; 7:156).
- unifies humanity by promoting gender and race equality. (49:13).
- values women (3:195; 4:124; 16:97).
- values intellect (5:90).
- offers peace among nations (2:62; 2:135-136, 208).
- considers the entire world as belonging to all humanity and supports immigration (4:97-98).
- promotes peace, while deterring the aggressive parties (60:8,9; 8:60).
- pursues the golden-plated brazen rule of equivalence, that is, retaliation with occasional forgiveness (42:20; 17:33).
- stands for human rights and the oppressed (4:75).
- encourages competition in righteousness and morality (16:90).
- stands for peace, honesty, kindness, and deterring from wrongdoing (3:110).
- expects high moral standards (25:63-76; 31:12-20; 23:1-11).
- asks us to be in harmony with nature and environment (30:41).
- teaches that the only system/law approved by god is Islam (3:19,85).

Through *hadith*, *sunna* and sectarian jurisprudence, scholars produced various sects, orders, or religions which were later attributed to their names (Shafii, Hanbali, Maliki, Hanafi, Jafari, Vahhabi, etc) to replace God's system of *Islam* or surrender and peace. The breadth and depth of distortion is astonishing. Here is a sample list of distortions made by the leaders of Sunni and Shiite sects, despite the Quranic teachings to the contrary. The list below is a selection of anti-Quranic teachings, which are found in the most respected Sunni or Shiite sources:

Teachings Based on the Man-Made Sources, Such As, *Hadith, Sunna, Ijma,* and *Sharia*[3]	The Quranic Verses Contradicting these Teachings, and Brief Discussions on Their Sources
Killing apostates, that is, those who leave Islam (read Sunni or Shiite), is commanded. Also anyone who verbally attacks or insults the prophet should be killed. Muhammad sent a platoon at night to kill a woman poet who criticized or insulted him. We are ordered to kill people until they declare "*la ilaha illa allah*" (there is no god but God)	Muhammad was not a tyrant. Islam promotes freedom of opinion, religion and expression. Muslims cannot use violence against even those who insult God (2:256; 4:140; 6:68; 10:99; 18:29; 88:21,22). Critical studies on the history of *hadith* shows the origins of intolerant teachings found in *hadith* books to the Jewish scholars who claimed to have converted to Islam. Our intention is not to accuse Jews for the corruption, but to show the similarities and the common origin of the corruption. According to the Quran, every individual will be held responsible from his or her choices. So, no Muslim can save themselves on the Day of Judgment by pointing at a Jewish reporter of hearsay for their own betrayal of the Quran. Even the Sunni and Shiite scholars acknowledge the great influence of Jewish teachings and practices have found their way into *hadith* and *sunna*. They called them *Israiliyyat* and wrote volumes of books to analyze and expose them. However, despite their efforts, still many of those teachings passed their poor and inconsistent filters. We are not claiming that the only source of violent teachings came from corrupt Jewish teachings, but the influence is one of the historically documented main factors. Here are a few examples of intolerance and cruel punishment attributed to God through Moses (The Quran refers to the distortions made in the Bible: 2:59; 2:79; 5:13-15; 5:41-44) for those who harbor different opinions or choose different religious beliefs: "The Lord said to Moses: 'Take the blasphemer outside the camp. All those who heard him are to lay their hands on his head, and the entire assembly is to stone him. Say to the Israelites: If anyone curses his God, he will be held responsible; anyone who blasphemes the name of the Lord must be put to death. The entire assembly must

---

[3]   Every sect does not necessarily subscribe to all of the following theological statements, but most are common belief catechisms among the major sects who have abandoned the Quran).

	stone him. Whether an alien or native-born, when he blasphemes the Name, he must be put to death.... Then Moses spoke to the Israelites, and they took the blasphemer outside the camp and stoned him. The Israelites did as the Lord commanded Moses." (Leviticus 24:13-16) "If your very own brother, or your son or daughter, or the wife you love, or your closest friend secretly entices you, saying, 'Let us go and worship other gods' ... Show him no pity. Do not spare him or shield him. You must certainly put him to death. Your hand must be the first in putting him to death, and then the hands of all the people. Stone him to death, because he tried to turn you away from the Lord your God, who brought you out of Egypt, out the land of slavery. Then all Israel will hear and be afraid, and no one among you will do such an evil thing again." (Deu 13:6-11) "Then shall thou bring forth that man or that woman, which have committed that wicked thing, unto thy gates, even that man or that woman, and shall stone them with stones, till they die." (Deuteronomy 17:5) "These are the statutes and judgments, which ye shall observe to do in the land, which the LORD God of thy fathers giveth thee to possess it, all the days that ye live upon the earth. Ye shall utterly destroy all the places, wherein the nations which ye shall possess served their gods, upon the high mountains, and upon the hills, and under every green tree: And ye shall overthrow their altars, and break their pillars, and burn their groves with fire; and ye shall hew down the graven images of their gods, and destroy the names of them out of that place." (Deuteronomy 12:2-4) The first five books of the Old Testament do not exactly correspond to the book given to Moses since they contain interesting clues about the distortions and additions made in the name of Moses. (Deuteronomy 34:5- 10; Numbers 12:3) Ironically, the Jews are no longer following these instructions, and many of them do have no desire to resurrect them. They left them to the followers of *hadith* and *sunna* who are dreaming a world based on those fabricated Jewish instructions. No wonder, the minds and attitude of a Jewish zealot and a Sunni zealot are much alike, like twins. Yet, they hate each other.
Those who do not observe daily prayers should be	The Quran mentions daily contact prayers about 70 times, and nowhere has it instructed us to beat or harass those who do not observe them. Contact prayers are to be observed for the one and

beaten in public.	only God (20:14). This rule is an assault on dignity, which God has bestowed on humanity (17:70) and promotes the observance of prayer for fear of social chastisement rather than for God, as they should be (6:162).
	The *hadith* reports again follow the Jewish tradition imposing severe penalties for those who commit sins or do not observe their expected religious rituals. For instance, those who violate the Sabbath, according to the Old Testament must be stoned to death (Numbers 15:32-36).
Married adulterers should be stoned to death *(al-rajm)*.	Stoning-to-death is never recommended in the Quran as a punishment for any crime. It was a Jewish practice which found its way into the practice of the so-called Muslims centuries after the revelation of the Quran, through *hadith* and *sunna*. The God who legislated a hundred lashes for married adulterers who accept the jurisdiction of Islam (24:1-10; 4:25) is the same God who made the Quran clear (24:1), who does not have any shortage of words (31:27), who is the best legislator (5:50), who does not forget (19:64), and who has detailed the Quran (11:1; 6:114; 12:111).
	Ironically, the word *rajm* is used in the Quran not for stoning but for rejecting and excommunicating. This is a common threat used by pagans against monotheists (11:91; 19:46; 36:18; 18:20).
	The Old Testament instructs a stoning-to-death penalty for various sins and crimes, including witchcraft; blasphemy, violating the Sabbath, and murder:
	"Again, thou shall say to the children of Israel, Whosoever he be of the children of Israel, or of the strangers that sojourn in Israel, that gives any of his seed unto Molech; he shall surely be put to death: the people of the land shall stone him with stones." (Leviticus 20:2)
	"A man also or woman that hath a familiar spirit, or that is a wizard, shall surely be put to death: they shall stone them with stones: their blood shall be upon them." (Leviticus 20:27)
	"And he that blasphemes the name of the LORD, he shall surely be put to death, and all the congregation shall certainly stone him: as well the stranger, as he that is born in the land, when he blasphemes the name of the LORD, shall be put to death." (Leviticus 24:16)
	"And the LORD said unto Moses, The man shall be surely put to death: all the congregation shall stone him with stones without the camp." (Numbers 15:35)
	"And if he smite him with throwing a stone, wherewith

he may die, and he die, he is a murderer: the murderer shall surely be put to death." (Numbers 35:17)

"But if this thing be true, and the tokens of virginity be not found for the damsel: Then they shall bring out the damsel to the door of her father's house, and the men of her city shall stone her with stones that she die: because she hath wrought folly in Israel, to play the whore in her father's house: so shalt thou put evil away from among you." (Deuteronomy 22:20-21)

Exodus chapter 21 has many more stoning-to-death instructions. Even animals get their share of this stoning penalty:

"If a bull gores a man or a woman to death, the bull must be stoned to death, and its meat must not be eaten." (Exodus 21:28)

According to the Old Testament, a rapist should be forced to marry the girl he violated. This rule punishes the victim to share the rest of her life with the violent and shameless man who violated her (Deuteronomy 22:28-30). How can this and many other unjust laws be imposed by a Just God?

There was a Quranic verse instructing stoning to death for married adulterers, but it was eaten by a hungry holy goat after Muhammad's death. Though these verses were abrogated through the goat, they are still legally binding and their meaning is valid.	This is an absurd lie. There is no abrogation in the Quran. 4:82; 6:21; 15:9; 15:90-99; 2:85; 6:19,38,43,112-115; 7:52; 10:15,37; 16:89; 18:27; 41:42.
Omar, the second Caliph, wanted to restore the Quran by reinserting the verses eaten by the goat; but he could not do it because of his fear of what	It is most likely a lie attributed to Omar. Regardless, the Quran is not left to be tempered by someone's decision, including Muhammad (15:9; 74:30; 41:41,42; 9:127; 75:17-19). A Muslim reveres God and is not afraid of what other people would say (3:175; 5:54; 32:16; 39:36; 50:45; 74:53).

14

people would say.	
Those who are caught consuming alcohol for the fourth time should be killed.	The Quran suggests society penalize crimes that incur injustice or harm another person; the Quran does not ask us to penalize immorality or personal sins. People may regulate or restrict the consumption of alcohol or drugs. This should not be done in the name of God, which gives it absolute power. Human experience shows that production, sales, and consumption of alcohol or drugs should not be prohibited by the society. People should have freedom to choose to be stupid, to commit sins, including the biggest one, which is, setting partners up with God (2:256; 18:29). It is no coincidence that we find many Jewish customs (such as circumcision), stories (such as ascension to the seventh heaven), penalties (such as stoning to death), etc., entering Islam through *hadith* narrations, since many Jewish scholars, became respected figures after their "conversion." Chapter 20 of Leviticus contains a list of very severe punishments for various sins. The severity of the prescribed punishments, however, is harsher and more diverse than what we find in *hadith*. The following examples will provide an insight regarding deformation. For instance, • cursing one's own father of mother would prompt death penalty; • a man marrying a woman together with her daughter must be burned in the fire. • homosexual men must be put to death. • people found guilty of bestiality, together with the animals must be put to death. And many more penalties of death. The following penalty prescribed by the Old Testament is both bizarre and unjust: "If two men are fighting and the wife of one of them comes to rescue her husband from his assailant, and she reaches out and seizes him by his private parts, you shall cut off her hand. Show her no pity." (Deuteronomy 25:11-12)
There were three Jewish tribes in Medina: Banu Qaynuqa, Banu al-Nadir and Banu Qurayza. They provoked Muslims and the first two tribes were forced	The Quran refers to the event and never mentions killing or enslaving them, which is in direct contradiction of many verses of the Quran. The Quran, in the Chapter known as Exodus, informs us that a group from "The People of the Book" were forced to leave the territory because of their violation of the constitution and secretly organizing war together with the enemies against Muslims (59:1-4). Verse 59:3 clearly states that they were not penalized further in this world.

to leave the city with their transportable possessions. However, prophet Muhammad did not forgive Banu Qurayza; their necks were struck and their children were made slaves. Estimates of those killed vary from 400 to 900.	The credibility of the story of Muhammad massacring Bani Qurayza Jews has been the subject of controversy since the time it was published by Ibn Ishaq. Ibn Ishaq who died in 151 A.H., that is 145 years after the event in question, was severely criticized by his peers for relying on highly exaggerated Jewish stories. He was also harshly criticized for presenting forged poetry attributed to famous poets. Some of his contemporary scholars, such as Malik, called him "a liar." However, his work was later copied by others without critical examination. This is an example of hearsay used by dubious reporters for propaganda purposes.
	Modern scholars found astonishing similarities between Ibn Ishaq and the account of the historian Josephus regarding King Alexander, who ruled in Jerusalem before Herod the Great, hung upon crosses 800 Jewish captives, and slaughtered their wives and children before their eyes. Many other similarities in details of the story of Banu Qurayza and the event reported by Josephus are compelling.
	Besides, the lack of reference or justification in the Quran for such a massacre of great magnitude and the verses instructing principles for Muslims to abide by removes all credibility from this story (35:18: 61:4). The Quran gives utmost importance to human life (5:32) and considers racism and anti-Semitism evil (49:11-13).
The prophet gave permission to kill children and women in war.	There is no such permission in the Quran. This instruction, which is used by Sunni or Shiite terrorists to justify their killing of innocent people for their cause, contradicts one of the most often repeated Quranic principles of not holding responsible one person for the crimes of another (6:164; 17:15; 35:18; 39:7; 53:38). The Quran, which condemns the ingrates for attacking weak men, women and children (4:75), would not justify the same action for Muslims.
	This and many other vicious instructions found in the so-called "authentic" *hadith* books, including Bukhari, had a major motive: to provide religious justification for aggression, atrocities, and massacres committed by the Umayyad and Abbasid kings and their governors.
	Another source of these instructions for violence and terrorism comes from Jewish literature, which found its way into *hadith* books through the Jewish scholars who supposedly converted to Islam. The Old Testament contains numerous instructions for violence and terror, which cannot be attributed to a benevolent and just God. They are mixed and introduced together with beautiful and constructive instructions:
	"And they devoted the city to the Lord and they utterly destroyed all that was in the city, both man and woman,

young and old, and ox, and sheep, and ass, with the edge of the sword." (Joshua 6:21)

"Now go and smite Amalek, and utterly destroy all that they have, and spare them not; but slay both man and woman, infant and suckling, ox and sheep, camel and ass." (1Samuel 15:3)

Also see the following verses from the Old Testament:

Exodus 22:18-19. Kill witches, perverts, polytheists.

Leviticus 20:1-27. Stone to death anyone gave offspring to Molech. Kill anyone cursing father or mother. Kill the adulterers. Kill homosexuals. Kill and burn those committing incest. Kill those who commit bestiality and their animals. Kill the fortune-tellers.

Leviticus 21:16-23. Lynch and stone the blasphemer to death.

Leviticus 24:13-18. Stone the blasphemer to death.

Numbers 15:32-36. Stone to death the man who collected sticks on the Sabbath.

Numbers 31:1-18. Children of Israel killed all the males of Midianites and took all the women of Midian captives, their little ones, their property. Then burned all their cities, and killed all the little boys.

Deuteronomy 13:6-10. Stone to death any of your relatives who serve the gods of other tribes.

Deuteronomy 17:2-7. Stone to death man or woman who served other gods after two or three witnesses testifies against them.

Deuteronomy 20:16-17. Kill every living being in the cities of Hittites, Amorites, Canaanites, Perizzites, Hivites, and Jebusites, and utterly destroy their cities.

Deuteronomy 22:23-24. Stone to death the adulterers.

Deuteronomy 25:11-12. Cut of a woman's hand if she holds the balls of another man while her husband is fighting with.

Joshua 6:20-21. Joshua and his men utterly destroyed all that was in the city, both man and woman, young and old, ox, sheep and ass, with the edge of the sword.

Judges 1:4-12. Judah killed ten thousand men from Canaanites and Perizzites; and cut off the thumbs and toes of their leaders. Judah fought against Jerusalem and set it on fire. Then, Judah slew Sheshai, Ahiman,Talmai, and then attacked the inhabitants of Debir.

Judges 3:22-29. The people of the Israel were saved by an assassin who deceptively reached to the King Eglon of Moab and stabbed him to death. Ehud led a gang of Israelis to Moab and killed 10,000 of their men.

1 Samuel 15:3. God sent Samuel to smite Amalek and utterly destroy all they have, sparing nothing, slaying both men and women, infant and suckling, ox and sheep, camel and ass.

2 Kings 2:23-24. When the little children of Bathel called Elisha 'baldhead' he cursed them and soon two bears came out and

	mauled 42 of the children.
	2 Chronicles 15:13. Whosoever would not seek the Lord God of Israel should be put to death, whether small or great, whether man or woman.
	Psalms 58:10-11. The righteous shall rejoice when he sees the vengeance: he shall wash his feet in the blood of the wicked.
	Psalms 137:9. Happy is he who dashes the infants of Babylon to the rocks.
	Psalms 149:6-9. Praise God and execute vengeance with a two edged sword against heathens.
	Isaiah 13:13-16. Their infants will be dashed to pieces before their eyes; their houses will be looted and their wives ravished.
	Jeremiah 48:10. Whoever keeps his sword from bloodshed is cursed.
	Jeremiah 51:10-24. Israel is God's battle axe and weapons of war. Ambush Babylon and destroy them to take vengeance. With Israel God will break the nations in pieces, will break the man and woman, the old and young in pieces,
	Ezekiel 9:5-6. Go to Jerusalem and kill, without showing pity or compassion. Slaughter old men, young men and maidens, women and children, but do not touch anyone who has the mark.
	Ezekiel 23:25. Israel's God will direct his jealous anger against Babylonians, Chaldeans, Pekod, Shoa, Koa, and the Assyrians, and they will be dealt with in fury. Their noses and ears will be cut off, and they will fall by the sword. Their sons and daughters will be taken, and those who are left will be consumed by fire.
	Zephaniah 3:8. The fire of God's jealous anger will consume the whole world.
	The New Testament, however, contains a different teaching. Nevertheless, since the New Testament relies on many verses of the Old Testament and there are ambiguities regarding the degree of its validity for Christians, Christians have justified many barbaric acts, atrocities, and torture by using and abusing the verses of both Old and New Testaments.
	• Mat 5:17-19, 29-30; • Mat 10:34; • Mat 19:12; • Mat 21:19; • John 15:6 (was abused by the church and used together with Exodus 22:18 to burn witches) • 1 Peter 2:13-14 (following this instruction, many atrocities and wars were committed by Christians)
When Muhammad was 53 years-old,	This is another lie by the enemies of God and His messenger. They tried to create a moon-splitting, tree-moving, child-crippling

he married Aisha who was only 9 years-old.	superman with the sexual power of 30 males (Verse 24:11-12 with its non-specific language, prophetically addresses this lie too). Muhammad was an honorable person and would not have a sexual relationship with a child (68:4; see 4:5-6). Discrepancies in the historical account show a deliberate attempt to reduce Aisha's age. This lie is perhaps produced to justify the sexual excesses of kings and the wealthy. They tried to justify their violence, oppression, injustice, sexual transgressions, and many other crimes through the fabrication and promotion of *hadith*.
The menstruating women should not touch the Quran, should not pray and should not enter the mosques.	This is based on a misunderstanding of at least two verses. Verse 56:79 is not an inscriptive but a descriptive verse about understanding of the Quran. The only verse mentioning menstruation forbids sexual intercourse during menstruation since it is considered a painful period (2:222), and does not forbid women from praying or reading the Quran. The Quran prohibits sexual relationship with a menstruating woman, not because she is dirty, but because menstruation is painful. The purpose is to protect women's health from being burdened by the sexual desires of their husbands. However, the male authors of the Old Testament, exaggerated and generalized this divine prohibition so much so that they turned menstruation to a reason for their humiliation, isolation, and punishment. (Leviticus 15:19-33) Despite the Quranic rule, the followers of *hadith* and *sunna* adopted Jewish laws that consider a woman unclean, and treat her like dirt for fourteen straight days of every month. According to the fabricated rules of the Old Testament, a menstruating woman is considered unclean for seven days, and during that period wherever she sits will be considered unclean; whoever touches her or sits where she sits must wash and bathe. After she finishes the menstruation, she has to wait for seven more days to be considered clean for ceremonial purposes. (Leviticus 15:19-33)
Women should not lead congregational prayers, and it is not recommended for them to participate either.	The verse instructing those who acknowledge the truth to gather for congregational prayer does not exclude women (62:9). The Quranic expression, "O you who acknowledge..." includes both men and women. Thank God, we have ended this misogynistic rule since 1999 and women have been leading congregational prayers and giving speeches ever since. The end of the world did not come, nor did anything bad happen. To the contrary, we are now blessed with being members of a balanced congregation.
Women are mentally and spiritually inferior	These are male chauvinist statements that reflect a diabolic arrogance, and lack appreciation of half of the human population,

to men.	who are the mothers, sisters, friends, and wives. (9:71; 33:35)
If a donkey, a dog, or a woman passes in front of the praying person the prayer is nullified. Hell will be filled with mostly women; women are deficient in intelligence and religion.	This is another misogynistic statement falsely attributed to Muhammad by so-called "authentic" *hadith* books. If we measure the level of intelligence by people's response to those who questioned their dogmas and superstitious beliefs, men have not scored better than women. Most of those who committed violence against the messengers and prophets were the male leaders, and most of those who distorted their message after their departure, again were all male religious leaders.

This is another misogynistic statement falsely attributed to Muhammad by so-called "authentic" *hadith* books. If we measure the level of intelligence by people's response to those who questioned their dogmas and superstitious beliefs, men have not scored better than women. Most of those who committed violence against the messengers and prophets were the male leaders, and most of those who distorted their message after their departure, again were all male religious leaders.

With a few exceptions based on biological differences or special conditions, men and women are considered equal in every aspect. The Quran expressly states the equality of man and woman, by the expression "you are from each other" (4:25). Furthermore, it reminds us of the common origin of both sexes and the purpose of why God created us as male and female, is the purpose being love and care (30:21). *Hadith* sources do not reflect a loving and caring relationship between man and woman, but an arrogant, chauvinistic and patronizing attitude towards women. Unfortunately, when consultation and election was replaced by monarchy and satanic *khilafa* (theocratic rule), the rights women enjoyed with the revelation of the Quran were taken one by one, and within two centuries after Muhammad, Muslims reverted to the misogynistic attitudes and practices of the pre-Islamic days of ignorance.

The rights of women during the time of prophet Muhammad is reflected with all its power in verse 58:1, where a Muslim woman argues with Muhammad regarding her husband. God does not reprimand that woman; to the contrary, God sides with the grievances of the woman and criticizes the superstition. A critical study of *hadith* and history books will reveal that even those books contain many hints regarding the individual, social and political rights enjoyed by women during the era of revelation and even decades afterwards. History books report that Aisha, Muhammad's wife, in her old age became the leader and commander of a major faction that participated in a civil war that took place thirty years after the departure of Muhammad.

Verse 60:12 informs us of the rights and privileges enjoyed by women in the early Muslim community during the life of Prophet Muhammad. In that verse, the prophet acknowledges women's right to vote, by taking the pledge of believing women to peacefully surrender themselves to God alone and lead a righteous life. The word "*BaYA*" used in the verse implies the political nature of the pledge; they accepted the leadership of the prophet individually, with their free choice. This verse is not about some pagan or *mushrik* women embracing Islam, but rather about a group of Muslim women publicly announcing their allegiance to Muhammad who became a founder of a federally secular constitutional government in central Arabia. This is a historical document that Muslim women were not considered default appendices of their decision-making husbands, brothers, fathers or male guardians, but Muslim women were treated as independent political entities who could vote and enter into social contract with their leaders. Unfortunately, many of the human rights recognized by Islam were later one by one taken away from individuals, especially from women, by the leaders of Sunni and Shiite religions; they replaced the progressive teaching of the Quran and practices of the early Muslims with hearsay fabrications thereby resurrecting the dogmas and practices of the days of ignorance. It took humanity centuries to grant women their God-given rights. For instance, the US recognized the right of women to vote in 1919 by passing the 19th Amendment, exactly, 13 centuries after it was recognized by the Quran. As for the region that once led the world in human rights and freedom, it is more than 13 centuries behind! After women, the men too lost their dignity to elect their leaders. What a regression!

According to the Quran, Mary was a sign for the world just as Jesus was (21:91). The Quran reports that Abraham's wife together with her husband welcomed male guests, participated in conversation, and laughed loud in their presence. She was not reprimanded for participating. To the contrary, at that meeting, God blesses her with the good news of pregnancy with Ishaq (11:71).

Verse 49:13 unequivocally rejects sexism and racism, and it reminds us that neither male nor female, neither this race nor that race is superior over the other. The only measure of superiority is righteousness; being a humble, moral and socially conscientious person who strives to help others.

The Quran is filled with verses referring to men and women in a neutral language that treats them equally (3:195; 4:7,25,32,124; 9:68-72; 16:97; 24:6-9; 33:35-36; 40:40; 49:13; 51:49; 53:45; 57.18; 66:10; 75:37-39; 92:3).

The Old Testament and St. Paul's Letters in the New Testament contain many misogynistic instructions. I recommend comparing Torrey's index for entries on 'Man' and 'Woman.' The comparison will show how the Old Testament and St. Paul are biased against women. St. Paul's misogynistic teaching is a reflection and extension of a historical trend. The Old Testament contains many man-made misogynist teachings. For instance, a woman is considered unclean for one week if she gives birth to a son, but unclean for two weeks if she gives birth to a daughter (Leviticus 12:1-5).

Here are some of the misogynistic Biblical verses that changed the so-called Muslims' attitudes towards women centuries after the

	Quran: • Woman was created from Adam's ribs (Genesis 2:21-22). • Woman was deceived by Satan (Genesis 3:1-6; 2 Corinthians 11:3; 1 Timothy 2:14). • Woman led man to disobey God (Genesis 3:6,11-12); • Woman was cursed (Genesis 3:16); • Woman is weaker than man (1 Peter 3:7); • Woman is subordinate to man (1 Corinthians 11:7).
Women should be covered from head to toe under a veil. Women should be confined in their homes. Women should be segregated in public places.	Societies, on certain occasions, times, or places might choose to segregate the sexes, but none can sanctify those decisions in the name of God. After a brief period of freedom and progress women enjoyed during the revelation of the Quran and several decades afterwards, they lost many of their human rights because of the fabricated misogynistic teachings introduced under the title of *hadith, sunna,* and sharia of various sects (3:195; 4:19,32; 9:71; 2:228). The word "*KHuMuR*" in 24:31 is a plural noun that comes from the root word of "*KHaMaRa*" which means, "to cover." It is used for any cover, not exclusively for headscarves. An extensive Arabic dictionary, *Lisan-ul Arab*, informs us that the word was even used for rugs and carpets, since they cover the floor. The singular form of the same word "*KHaMR,*" has been used for intoxicants, which "cover" the mind (5:90). In verse 24:31, God advises female Muslims to maintain their chastity and put their covers on their chests, not their heads! Additionally, the word "*fel yedribne* = they shall put, they shall cover" is significant in that verse. If *KHuMuR* meant head cover, the verb, "*fel yudnine* = they shall lengthen," (like in 33:59) would be more appropriate. Another distortion involves the word "*ZiYNa*" of verse 24:31. Muslim clergymen have abused this word to cover women from head to toe. They considered almost all parts of female body as *ZiYNa*. Reflecting on the rituals of ablution for the daily prayers, one can easily infer that women can publicly open their faces, hair, arms, and feet as an act of worship (5:6). Therefore, opening their faces and arms is indeed an act of worship; and they are not required to worship in secret or segregated places (17:110). If a man stares at a woman who is taking ablution and is sexually aroused it is not her fault, but it is either a symptom of his psychological problems or an indication of the deep-rooted problems in that society. By requiring women to cover any of these parts of their body, religious scholars have turned a religious ritual into a matter of sexual expression. It is up to women to cover themselves for their own protection. It is not up to men or moral police to mandate or impose this divine

instruction on women, since the instruction is personal and specific to women. Besides, the language of the instruction is deliberately designed to accommodate different cultures, norms, conditions, and individual comfort level. A divine recommendation to protect women from the harassment of unrighteous men should not be abused to justify the harassment and oppression of self-righteous misogynistic men.

Verse 33:52 informs us that Muhammad was attracted to the physical beauty of women. No reasonable man is attracted to the "beauty" of women walking in black sacks. Despite this verse informing us that Muslim women during the time of Muhammad were interacting with men, their faces open, those who tried to deprive women from social and political life and from their individual and group identity went to the extreme and issued religious *fatwas* mandating a veil to cover their faces. The veil is a satanic innovation designed to turn women into the slaves of men who claim to be lords and masters.

Verse 60:12 mentions the practice of another role model, prophet Muhammad. Muhammad did not receive any divine warning regarding the danger of the devil during this face-to-face interaction! Furthermore, the Quran permits men and woman to eat together or to help each other (24:61; 3:195; 9:71).

The Quran, for important political reasons, advises to the wives of the Prophet not to mingle with people as they used to (33:32-33). The advice is due to protecting Muhammad and his spouses from the defamation campaign started by the unappreciative crowd (8:30-31; 24:11-20).

Ironically, the followers of *hadith* ignore their own history regarding the condition of women during the time of Muhammad and the four "guide leaders": Aisha, Muhammad's wife, is reported to lead a faction of Muhammad's companions after his departure. How could have Aisha lead men and women, in peace and war, if she did not interact and communicate with them, if she did not have her own identity, if she was imprisoned in her home or in her black veil?

The Quran provides several examples of women being active role models in their societies and interacting with men, such as Abraham's wife (11:69-71; 60:4-6), Muslim women in Madyan with one whom Moses married (28:23-28), the Queen of Sheba who later surrenders to the will of God (27:34:40), and Mary (19:16-30; 3:42-43; 66:11-12). Muslim women were so outspoken that they could engage in debate with Muhammad (58:1), and women pledged allegiance and voted for Muhammad's leadership (60:12).

Therefore, segregating men and women has no Islamic basis; it is a un-Quranic practice imported from misogynistic teachings of St.

	Paul and the Old Testament.
	Segregation in places of worship existed as an innovation among Jews (Exodus 38:8; 1 Samuel 2:22) and reached its zenith with additional condemnation and degradation with St. Paul who condemned women for Adam's sin and silenced them in the public arena.
	"Let your women keep silent in the churches, for they are not permitted to speak; but they are to be submissive, as the law also says." (I Corinthians 14: 34)

"For a woman is not covered, let her also be shorn. But if it is shameful for a woman to be shorn or shaved, let her be covered. For a man indeed ought not to cover his head, since he is the image and glory of God; but woman is the glory of man. For man is not from woman, but woman from man. Nor was man created for the woman, but woman for the man." (I Corinthians 11:6-9)

"Let a women learn in silence with all submission. And do not permit a woman to teach or to have authority over a man, but to be in silence. For Adam was formed first, then Eve. And Adam was not deceived, but the woman being deceived, fell into transgression. Nevertheless, she will be saved in childbearing if they continue in faith, love and holiness, with self-control." (I Timothy 2:11-15) |
	The followers of *hadith* and *sunna* adopted the misogynistic teachings of St. Paul, and still many of them clung onto them as their religion, while most of Christendom has meanwhile mutated many times and quietly ignored and abandoned those teachings. In the Christian world, St. Paul's teachings have been partially rejected; women no longer cover their heads, and they no longer stay silent in churches. It is ironic that today's Sunnis and Shiites follow more seriously many of the teachings of Judaism and Christianity than the Jews and Christians themselves.
A woman cannot divorce her husband on her own.	Verse 2:228 establishes equal rights to both genders. By associating and even preferring numerous collections of lies and innovations to the Quran, the followers of *hadith* and *sunna* denied Muslim women the right to divorce and turned them into slaves of male despotism.
A man can divorce his wife by uttering some words three	Sectarian scholars who ignored the Quran and upheld volumes of books of *hadith* and *sunna*, issued laws (*sharia*) allowing the marriage contract to be terminated with several words coming

24

times.	from the husband's mouth. Divorce is an event lasting several months; it is not just an oral declaration of the male spouse. A wife cannot be divorced by announcing, "I divorce you three times." This ease and one-sided divorce created miserable marriages and destroyed many families. Many men, who "divorced" their wives by uttering the magical word "*talaq*" (divorce) unintentionally or in the heat of anger, desperately looked for a solution (*fatwa*), and found mullahs and religious judges selling *fatwas* to save their marriage! The class that created the problem in the first place became the benefactor of the solution (2:226-230; 9:34-35; 33:49).
	The New Testament takes the opposite direction; divorce is considered a great offense and after the marriage, none should divorce, except for reasons of adultery. Marriage after divorce is committing adultery (Matthew 5:32; 19:9).
Polygamy up to four women is permitted. One can marry four previously unmarried women. Men do not need the consent of his wife(s) for polygamy.	The Quran does not limit the number of women. Though the Quran allows polygamy (4:3), it discourages its practice by requiring certain conditions: a man can marry more than one, only to the widows with children and should try to treat them equally (4:19-20, 127-129). Besides the consent of the former wife(s) is essential since they have the right to object or divorce their husbands. Unfortunately, verse 4:127 has been traditionally mistranslated as to allow marriage with juvenile orphans rather than their mothers. The word "*ibkar*" in verse 66:5 too has been mistranslated. For discussion on verses, 4:127 and 66:5 please see the notes.
	It is an injustice to blame the Quran for advising us to care about the orphaned children and their widowed mothers. These verses primarily advocate the economic interests, psychological and biological needs, and social status of orphans, especially during war. Unfortunately, the enemies of the last prophet who attributed volumes of fabrications to him (6:112-116), have distorted the meaning and purpose of these wonderful divine precepts.
	Muhammad's marriages to widows had political and social reasons. Unfortunately, the permission for polygamy was distorted and it became a means to satisfy the libido of the rich and dominant males. The all-male scholars, to achieve their goal used *hadith* and distorted the meaning of verses, such as 4:3-6, 4:127 and 66:5.
	Here, we should note that exaggerated examples of polygamy, explicit details of sexual affairs, and stories of incest have been inserted into the Bible. We find much similarity between stories in *hadith* books and those Biblical stories. For instance, 1 King 11:3 claims that Solomon had 700 wives and 300 concubines. Anyone familiar with the current versions of the Bible would know that it

	contains numerous textual problems, translational errors, and contradictions. Numbers in the Bible are easily subjected to distortion, exaggeration, or simple scribing errors. For instance, we see a big difference in the number of charioteers killed by David. It is 700 according to II Samuel 10:18 and it is 7000 according to I Chronicles 19:18. Note that both numbers are whole numbers and the discrepancy is ten times. A little attention to the numbers of wives and concubines attributed to Solomon would reveal a deliberate attempt to make it as round as possible. 700+300=1000. Total of seven zeroes! Most likely Solomon had a few wives. Contrary to the Quran that exhorts muslims to help widows, the misogynistic Rabbinical teachings inserted to the Old Testament put them in the category of harlots, and finds them unworthy of marriage by the privileged class, priests (Leviticus 21:14).
Dividing into sects is a good thing, as long as they are authorized by kings and their paid scholars.	Between Shiite and Sunni sects and among many branches of each sect, there are numerous contradictory rules. History is full of fights and persecution by one sect against another. Division into sects and factions is a symptom of ignorance and polytheism (3:19; 3:64,84-85; 6:159; 23:52-56; 30:32; 42:13-14; 68:36-38).
Pilgrims must cast stones at the devil.	Every year hundreds of pilgrims are killed and injured while an agitated crowd stampedes each other to death trying to cast stones and their shoes at a pillar representing Satan. The practice of stoning the devil during pilgrimage comes from the distortion made in the meaning of the word *rajm*. According to the Quran, God indeed did *'rajm'* Satan. The word *rajm*, according to the Quran, does not necessarily mean 'stoning,' but rather means 'rejecting' or 'excommunicating.' God did not stone Satan to death but excommunicated or rejected him from His presence. The word *rajm* simply means excommunication or rejection (3:36; 11:91; 15:17,34; 16:98; 18:20; 19:46; 26:116; 44:20; 36:18; 38:77; 81:25). It also means casting, forecasting, and throwing (18:22; 67:5). We are not sure when the meaning of *rajm* started including "stoning." Even if it had that extra meaning, it is obvious that cannot be the one considered in connection with Satan.
A Muslim may own slaves or concubines.	The widely practiced slavery was abolished by the Quran (3:79; 4:3,25,92; 5:89; 8:67; 24:32-33; 58:3-4; 90:13; 2:286; 12:39-42; 79:24). The Quran rejects slavery not as one of the big sins, but as the greatest sin and crime, equivalent of setting up partners to God, which is an unforgivable sin if maintained until death. The Quran unequivocally rejects accepting other than God as

lord/master (*rabb*). Claiming to be the lord/master of someone is tantamount to claiming to be God (12:39-40; 3:64; 9:31). Decades after Muhammad's departure kings and their accomplice religious leaders wanted to resurrect and justify slavery by distorting the verses about Joseph's reference to his friend's master (12:41,42). However, they ignored the fact that Joseph never called anyone other than God as his lord or master, and he advised his prison mates to seek freedom by rejecting the unjust claim of false lords/masters on them (12:39-40).

Verse 16:75-76 compares a slave with a free person and emphasizes the importance of being a free person. No wonder, the Quran condemns Pharaoh for his claim of being the lord and master of other people (79:15-26). God saved the Jews from slavery and reminded them that their freedom was more important than the variety of foods they were missing (2:57-61). The Quran warns Muhammad not to capture and imprison his enemies during peacetime, and gives him permission for such only as a measure against those who participate in war (8:67). The Quran acknowledges the fact that those who set up partners with God had slaves (24:32; 16:75), and freeing them is considered an activity and a quality of muslims (90:13).

It is ironic that Jews who suffered the most from slavery and were saved by God through the leadership of Moses (Exodus 1:13-14), later justified enslaving other people, including selling one's own daughter, and inserted that practice into their holy books (Exodus 21:7-8; 21:21-22; 26-27; Leviticus 25:44-46; Joshua 9:6-27).

Though Jesus never condoned slavery, St. Paul, the founder of modern Christianity, once asked the masters to treat their slaves nicely (Colossians 3:22), and asked the slaves to be "submissive to your masters with all fear" (1 Peter 2:18; Ephesians 6:5; 1 Timothy 6:2; Colossians 3:22; Titus 2:9) justifying the Marxist maxim, "Religion is the opium of masses." The use of religion by the privileged class to enslave or exploit people is vividly depicted by the Jomo Kenyatta, the first president of Kenya: "When the missionaries came to Africa, they had the Bible and we had the land. They said 'let us close our eyes and pray'. When we opened them, we had the Bible, and they had the land."

We should emulate prophet Muhammad and his companions and follow the details in *sharia* books that cover every aspect of one's life, from praying to sleeping,	This mindset makes a mockery of God's system. The Quran reports the message and struggle of numerous prophets, messengers and their supporters and nowhere do we see any word or discussion on how to groom one's hair and beards, how to cut nails, how to sleep, how to go to the bathroom, or any other formalities and trivial personal or cultural choices (5:101; 42:21; 2:67-71). While *hadith* books are filled with hundreds of contradictory narrations indulging in details of grooming, fashion, attire, even the color of clothes, the Quran reminds us not to focus

from cutting one's fingernails to going to the bathroom. Wearing a turban and growing beards in a particular fashion is a religious practice emulating Muhammad.	on these trivial issues, but focus on righteous deeds (7:26). Ironically, the Sunnis and Shiites do not even follow their *hadith* and *sunna* books consistently. Though *hadith* books describe Muhammad with long hair, almost all Sunni clerics who consider aping Muhammad as a path to eternal salvation cut their hair short like Buddhist monks. This is an anomaly for those who split hair in the name of Muhammad.

Circumcision is a religious practice needed to correct the male genitals.	Making changes in God's creation for religious purposes is considered evil (4:119). Obviously, foreskin is not an abnormality in God's creation; it is the norm. Attempting to change such a creation through surgery to attain salvation is superstition.
	
	The Quran never mentions Abraham practicing circumcision. If indeed Abraham did such a surgery on himself, perhaps he wanted to eliminate some kind of infection and the blind followers who later idolized him turned his personal deed into a religious ritual. Considering the history of Jewish people and their trials and tribulations, it is more likely that this is an invention of Rabbis, perhaps to mark the endangered race and protect it from extinction. Introducing innovations in religious communities may need some "holy stories" to attribute the innovation to historical idols.
	
	The Quran never mentions the adventures of the Biblical character Samson who had a bizarre hobby of collecting the foreskins of thousands of people he killed by the jaw of an ass (Old Testament Judges 15:16).
	
	The Old Testament contains hyperbolic exaggerations and bizarre practices. For instance, ignoring the discrepancy in the number of mutilated penises read the following verses from the Bible:
	
	    "So David rose and he and his men went and struck down among the Philistines two hundred men, and David came bringing their foreskins and giving them in full number to the king, to form a marriage alliance with the king. In turn Saul gave him Michal, his daughter, as a wife." (1 Samuel 18:27)
	
	    "Then David sent messengers to Ish-Bosheth son of Saul, demanding, 'Give me my wife Michal, whom I engaged to myself for a hundred foreskins of the Philistines." (2 Samuel 3:14)
	
	Using a bundle of foreskins of mutilated genitals of the dead bodies of an enemy as the symbolic show of manhood, and

	literally using them in exchange for a woman is difficult to digest. The Quran does not contain any of the Jewish insults to the Jewish prophets, such as David, Solomon, Lot, etc. Samson's obsession and adventure with Philistine girls is similarly strange (Judges 14). When Samson is betrayed by his wife, Timnah, or his heifer (Judges 14:18!), he loses the bet during the seven days of the feast. This time thirty men from Ashkelon have to lose their lives. Later, Samson torches Philistine grain fields with torches tied to the tails of foxes, kills a thousand Philistines with a "donkey's jawbone," and prays to God not to let him die in the hands of the "uncircumcised" (Judges 15:15-16). This Biblical hero, in his bloody pursuit of another wife, spends a night with a prostitute (Judges 16:1) and later another wife, Delilah, who shaves his hair, the source of his extraordinary power, thus betraying him (Judges 16:18-20). Samson dies after killing more Philistines. The story can be outlined in several words: Marriage, Feast, Foreskins, Slaughtering, Torching, Betraying, Heifer, Prostitute, Hairy Superstition, Killing, and Killing more! Muslims, long after the revelation of the Quran and departure of Muhammad, acquired from Jews the bizarre obsession with hair and foreskins! If someone converts to Sunni or Shiite religions, one of the first troubles he finds himself in is to undergo surgery on the foreskin of his penis and a holy recommendation to grow a long beard. Additionally, he will exchange his original name with an Arabic name! This is just the beginning of becoming a Jewish Arab who follows a concocted culture from the medieval ages.
Converts should change their names to Arabic names.	The names with negative meanings or implications should be changed, of course, but changing names to Arabic has no Quranic basis. No language is exclusively holy. To the contrary, diversity of languages is considered a divine blessing (30:22). Employing *hadith and sunna*, Arab nationalists of Umayyad and Abbasid era introduced their culture as Islam. Many converts experience personal dilemma and pass through an unnecessary pain by denying their non-Arabic names, which in most cases as beautiful as and sometimes more beautiful than the Arabic ones. This practice contradicts even the teachings of *hadith* and *sunna*. According to both Sunni and Shiite sources, those who converted to Islam from polytheism during the time of Muhammad never changed their names. Bilal of Ethiopia remained Bilal; Salman of Persia remained Salman, Omar remained Omar, Hamza remained Hamza. The same is true with all other prophets and messengers whose names are mentioned in the Quran. None of our role models changed their names to Arabic or to any other language. How can one consider human names in a particular language holy while God Almighty permits us to call him with any good

	attribute (17:110)?
Paying the *zakat* charity is required only once a year. There are many different rates for different assets and one must refer to his or her particular sect to find out how much *zakat* charity is due.	Purification of God's blessings, including the financial ones, through sharing them with others, is a continuous and important act of charity (6:141; 7:156). The amount of financial charity to the poor and needy is not fixed; it is left to individuals to decide based on certain guidelines (2:219; 17:29).
The Hajj pilgrimage should be done only on certain days.	Hajj pilgrimage can be done within four restricted months, *Zil Hijja, Muharram, Safar,* and *Rabi Awwal* (2:189,197).
Those who break their fast during Ramadan before the sunset should fast 60 more days for not completing the day as a punishment.	There is no such a penalty in the detailed, clear, and easy-to-understand book of the One who neither forgets, nor runs out of words (2:184).
Khalifa, that is succession in leadership, is the right of the Quraysh tribe.	No affair can be more deserving of consultation than the election of leaders. The Quran leaves this important issue to be decided by consultation or vote by the population (42:38). Muhammad was elected as a revolutionary leader by those who accepted his message on their own free will. After Muhammad, the election continued for about thirty years with the elections of Abu Bakr, Omar, Ali, and Usman. Usman's weakness and nepotism lead the Umayyad tribe to take over. Thus, the democratic system, which started with Muhammad, was replaced with monarchy several decades after his departure.
Gold and silk is prohibited for men.	Gold and silk is not prohibited for use by men. Prohibiting God's blessings in the name of God is the greatest sin (5:48-49; 6:145-150; 7:31-32; 10:59-60; 18:31; 22:23; 35:33; 42:21).
Drawing pictures of animated creatures,	This is another reflection of a shallow understanding of monotheism. The Quran does not prohibit drawing or making 3-D

and making their statutes is a great sin.	models of living beings. Prophet Solomon, who had statutes in his mansion, was a monotheist (34:13; 42:21).
Playing musical instruments other than those used by medieval Arabs is a sin.	The Quran contains many verses condemning the temptation of the religious people to prohibit the blessings of God (6:145-150; 7:31-32; 10:59-60; 42:21).
Dogs, especially black dogs, are from devil. If a dog touches you, you must wash in a special way.	This is another superstition reflecting the attitude of the *hadith* fabricator against a particular dog. *Hadith* books contain contradictory *hadiths*. Some well-respected narrators of the same sources accused Abu Hurayra of fabricating prohibitions. The Quran treats dogs as human companions, and mentions a dog as one of the members of the young monotheists who were protected from the oppression via a miraculous hibernation in a cave (18:18-22). Dogs may also be used in hunting, and their mouth does not make the game unclean (5:4).
Eating the meat of certain animals is prohibited and the contradictory list of prohibitions in authorized sects is good. The taste of the Quraysh tribe is the ultimate authority regarding which food is prohibited or not.	Despite the enumerated list given in the Quran and despite its clear rejection of any other dietary prohibitions, those who associated partners with God came up with additional and contradictory lists of prohibitions (6:145-150; 16:115-116; 42:21).
People cannot make it to heaven without accepting or uttering Muhammad's messengership. Testifying to the oneness of God is not enough without adding Muhammad's name.	The only requirement for attaining eternal salvation is to acknowledge one God, the hereafter, and live a righteous life (2:62; 5:69). Oneness of God is repeated as "*lailahe illallah*" or "*lailahe illa hu*" (there is no god but the God) thirty times in the Quran, and not a single time is it used in conjunction with Muhammad's name (3:18; 37:35; 38:65; 39:45; 47:19). Ironically, the only testimony (*shahada*) that includes Muhammad's name is attributed to hypocrites (63:1).

The black stone at the *Ka'ba* in Mecca has come from heaven and it should be respected. Visiting Muhammad's tomb in Medina is also a recommended religious duty on pilgrims.	The story about the black stone is a myth. Showing such a reverence to a stone or a tomb and asking for help from the dead is idolatry (1:5; 2:24; 10:106; 6:56; 7:194-197; 18:52; 22:73; 26:69-74; 28:88; 35:14,40; 39:38; 40:66; 46:5; 72:18; 2:149-150; 5:3; 16:120; 22:78; 66:6).
Muhammad's name and the names of his closest companions may be displayed next to God's name in mosques.	Muhammad did not come to replace his name with the names of previous idols. Putting Muhammad's name, or his close companions and relatives next to God is obviously an innovation of the hero-worshippers (17:110-111; 20:14; 72:18-19). Meccan polytheists did not have statues or concrete idols, as claimed in *hadith* books, rather they considered themselves followers of Abraham, the legendary monotheist. Thus, like today's Sunnis, Shiites and Christians they created more of an abstract idolization, through holy names, intercession and man-made religious laws (53:23).
We should pray to God alone while we are standing in *sala* prayers, but when we sit down we should call Muhammad as he is alive, omnipresent, and omniscient by addressing him "*essalamu alayKA ayyuha al-nabiyyu*" (o prophet, peace be upon YOU).	This is an obvious innovation, since Muhammad could not have uttered these words in his prayers; unless he were a schizophrenic (35:14, 40; 4:101-103; 29:45). In *sala* prayers, we should only commemorate God, declare our allegiance to Him and ask for His help. In prayer telling God the story of Moses and Pharaoh or the rules of inheritance, description of paradise and hell, etc., is not proper (17:110-111; 20:14; 72:18-19).
The consensus of religious scholars should be considered God's religion.	Though the number of votes in democratic societies is a valuable tool to determine the interest and the will of a population, the number of votes does not and should not determine the truth in scientific, philosophical, and theological matters. The teaching of Islam was completed by the end of the Quranic revelation (5:3; 6:114; 9:31-34).

Muhammad is the last messenger.	Muhammad was the last prophet (*nabi*) who brought the last testament, but he was not the last messenger (*rasul*) (3:81; 7:35; 33:7; 33:40; 72:7). The Quran gives the example of ingrates in the past who deprived themselves from receiving God's message and mercy by claiming the same thing (40:28-44).
Muhammad was an illiterate man and remained illiterate until his death.	Muhammad was a literate gentile (96:1-5; 68.1-10; 2:78; 3:20; 3:75; 7:157; 62:2; 2:44).
Muhammad advised some sick people to drink camel urine as a cure and then tortured a group of people accused of murdering his shepherd by gouging their eyes with hot nails, chopping off their arms and legs and leaving them in the desert dying from thirst.	Muhammad was a kind, tolerant and caring leader, not a torturer (3:159; 6:54; 21:107; 68:4). His advising camel urine as a medicine is highly doubtful (7:157). Even if he did advise such a thing, it would only reflect his cultural upbringing and lack of knowledge in the field of medicine.
God initially required us to pray 50 times (not units, times) a day when Muhammad met God in the seventh heaven during his *Miraj* (ascension). But, thankfully Moses, who was residing in the sixth heaven, repeatedly advised Muhammad to ask for more reduction in prayer. By oscillating between God in seventh	This is the longest story in *hadith* books, taking pages and pages, and it contains the fingerprints of Jewish storytellers. God never burdens a person beyond his or her capacity (2:286; 6:152; 7:42; 23:62). Claiming that God initially wished to impose prayer on people 50 times a day, which means one prayer for every 28 minutes, day and night, is denial of God's compassion. This story also insults Muhammad's intelligence, yet turns him into someone like a union leader negotiating on behalf of his people against a cruel boss, with Moses as the advisor. Moreover, *sala* prayer did not start with Muhammad; it started with Abraham (17:1,78; 53:1-182:83; 2:124-125; 2:238; 11:114; 24:58).

heaven and Moses in the sixth five times, Muhammad haggled for further discount of the numbers of prayers.	
Muhammad has the power of intercession and will save us on the Day of Judgment. Muhammad has the "highest" rank above all messengers.	None has the power of saving criminals from God's judgment. The Quran considers the faith in intercession of someone to be *shirk* or polytheism. If there is any intercession it will be a testimony for the truth (2:48,123,254; 6:70,94; 7:53; 10:3; 20:109; 34:23; 39:44; 43:86; 74:48; 78:38). Ironically, the Quran informs us that Muhammad will complain about his people deserting the Quran, not "his *sunna*" as they claim (25:30). Muhammadans are so ignorant and arrogant, like their ancestors they too are in denial of their associating partnership to God via attributing the power of intercession or other false powers to God's servants (6:23-26; 16:35; 39:3, 38; 19:81-82).
	Those who acknowledge Quran do not favor one messenger over another (2:285); all the messengers belong to the same community (21:92; 23:51-53)
	The Quran gives examples of many idolized concepts and objects. For instance, children (7:90), religious leaders and scholars (9:31), money and wealth (18:42), angels, dead saints, messengers and prophets (16:20,21; 35:14; 46:5,6; 53:23), ego/wishful thinking (25:43, 45:23) can all be idols.
	In order to infect the human mind with the most dangerous disease called *shirk* (associating partners to God, or polytheism), Satan infects the unappreciative minds with a virus to destroy the faculty of self-criticism by installing a faulty and defective recognition program. Therefore, most of those who associate partners with God in various ways do not recognize their polytheism (6:23). Polytheists show all the symptoms of hypnosis, their master hypnotist being Satan (6:22-24,43,110-113; 7:17,27-30,64-65,179; 10:42-43; 15:12-15,42; 16:35; 18:21,22,57; 17:45; 31:21; 47:16; 58:18-19; 59:16-19).
Uttering the name of Muhammad alone is disrespectful to Muhammad and deprives a person from his intercession. We should utter words	We are instructed to glorify and praise God (3:41; 3:191; 33:42; 73:8; 76:25; 4:103), not His messengers, who are only human beings like us. We are instructed by the Gracious and Merciful God to utter the name of messengers with their first names, without glorifying them, and Muhammad is no different from other messengers (2:136; 2:285; 3:144). Muhammad was a human being like us (18:110; 41:6), and his name is mentioned in the Quran as "Muhammad," similar to how other people are mentioned in the Quran (3:144; 33:40; 47:2; 48:29). Uttering an

of praise or distinguishing phrases, such as "*sallallahu alayhi wasallam*" or "Peace be Upon Him" whenever Muhammad's name is uttered. When with a congregation, we should show our respect to him by words or gestures whenever his name is mentioned.	expression containing "*salli ala*" after Muhammad's name is based on distortion of the meaning of a verb demanding action of support and encouragement of a living messenger, rather than utterance of praise for a dead messenger (compare 33:56 to 33:43; 9:103; and 2:157). Despite these verses clarifying the meaning of the word; despite the fact that the Quran does not instruct us to say something, but to do something; despite the fact that the third person pronoun in the phrase indicates that it was an innovation after Muhammad's departure; despite these and many other facts, Sunni and Shiite clerics try hard to find an excuse to continue this form of Muhammad-worship. Contradicting the intention and practice of masses, some clerics even claim this phrase to be a prayer for Muhammad rather than a phrase for his praise. Muhammad, especially the Muhammad of their imagination, should be the last person who would need constant prayers of millions. According to them, Muhammad has already received the highest rank in paradise, and again according to them he did not commit any sins. Therefore, the address of their prayers is terribly wrong. They should pray for themselves, for each other, not Muhammad. It is like homeless people donating their money, several times a day, to the richest person in the world. It is just as absurd.
Muhammad did not commit any sin. He was always a monotheist, on the right path.	Muhammad was a fallible human being. Before receiving the revelation, he followed the tradition of his people and he associated partners to God (4:79; 9:117; 33:37; 40:66; 42:52; 66:1; 80:1-10; 93:7). If he were a monotheist, God would not depict him being ignorant of *iman* (acknowledgement/faith) before the revelation of the Quran. History books claiming his popularity before the revelation of the Quran supports this Quranic fact. Ignorant polytheists whose theocratic system run by fanatically religious leaders would not respect a monotheist.
God created the universe for the sake of Muhammad.	The universe was not created for a specific person (14:33; 16:12; 31:29; 51:56).
Muhammad showed many miracles, including splitting the moon. According to some narrations, half of the moon fell in Ali's backyard.	Muhammad did not demonstrate any miracle; except the Quran (29:50-51). The splitting of the moon mentioned in the Quran is a prophetic description of splitting the soil of the moon in 1969 (54:1-2; see 80:26 ad 50:44 for the range of the meaning of "*shaqqa*"). The year 1969 is the start of the computer study that led to the discovery of the mathematical miracle of the Quran based on the number 19 of chapter 74 in year 1974 (74:1-56).

Muhammad was not a human being like us; he was a superman. He had sexual intercourse with nine women in a single night. Muhammad had the sexual power of 30 males.	The *hadith* fabricators were in fact the enemies of the prophet, as those Pauline Christians were the enemies of Jesus (6:112-116). *Hadith* fabricators depicted Muhammad to justify their fantasies. Another motive was to fabricate as many "miracles" as possible for the idolized Muhammad, including sexual miracles, to help him win the "competition" with other messengers mentioned in the Quran. Muhammad was a human being like us; he was not a superman (33:21; 18:110; 41:6).
Muhammad was bewitched by a Jew, and he wandered in the streets of Medina in utter confusion for weeks.	Muhammad was not bewitched; this claim was made by the ingrates who rejected his message (17:47; 25:8-10).
Muhammad died poor, so poor that he pawned his personal belongings to a Jew for a little barley	Once an orphan and poor, by God's blessing, Muhammad became a successful international wealthy merchant (93:8).
Each companion of prophet Muhammad is like a star and their actions and fatwas have authority in religious guidance.	Centuries after Muhammad, he and his companions became idols. The so-called Muslims started considering the prophet's companions (*sahaba*) or anyone who met him as a Muslim to be almost infallible, though some of his companions considered each other hypocrites. There are collections of hearsay attributed to these people (*akhbar*) and their words, comments, and speculations are considered another authority after *hadith*. The word *sahib, sahaba*, and its plural *ashab* are usually used in a negative context. For instance, out of the 77 occurrences of *ashab*, and the one occurrence of "*ashabahum*" (their comrades), only 27 are used positively, such as, "*ashab ul-Jannah*" (People of the Paradise) or "*ashab ul-Yameen*" (People of the Right). Excluding the few neutral usages of the word, the word "*ashab*" is usually used to denote ingrates and hypocrites. None of these *ashab*, the plural of *sahaba*, refers to Muslims who lived during time of Prophet Muhammad. In only one case, the plural *ashab* refers to people with Moses (26:61), and we learn from the Quran that most of them were not acknowledging the truth (7:138-178; 20:83-87).

Among the 12 occurrences of the singular and dual form, *sahib*, only five describe a relationship between a prophet and his friends. And, out of these five occurrences, only one of them has a positive connotation. Before quoting the verses, I want to remind you that the word *sahib* (companion, friend) is about a mutual relationship; if someone is your companion you are their companion too, and vice versa. In the following four occurrences, the addressees are opponents or polytheists:

> " . . Your companion (*sahib*) is not crazy. He is a profound Warner to you, just before the advent of a terrible retribution." (34:46)

> "Your companion (*sahib*) has neither strayed, nor is he deceived." (53:2)

> "Your companion (*sahib*) is not crazy." (81:22)

> "O my prison companions (*sahibay* = two companions), are separate lords better than God Alone, the Irresistible?" (12:39)

The only positive usage of the word *sahib*, as a companion of a Prophet is:

> ." . . Thus, when the ingrate chased him, and he was one of two in the cave, he said to his friend, 'Do not worry, God is with us.' . . ." (9:40)

In summary, according to the Quranic literature, the words *sahib* (companion) or *ashab* (companions) by themselves do not have any positive meaning. In three verses Muhammad is described as "*sahib* of ingrates" and in one verse, he was the companion of an acknowledging person.

In numerous verses, however, the Quran informs us about the quality of Muhammad's comrades (48:29). What we see, is not a depiction of perfect holy people, but ordinary people, with all sorts of weaknesses and shortcomings.

According to the books of *hadith*, Abdullah Ibn Masood was one of the top companions of the prophet. His *hadith* narrations are among Sunni Muslim's most cherished sources of jurisprudence. Many *hadith* and narration books, including Bukhari and Ibn Hanbal, report that Ibn Masood had a personal copy of the Quran and he did not put the last two chapters in it. According to those books, he claimed that those two chapters did not belong in the Quran.

Apparently, another companion of the prophet, Ubayy Ibn Kaab, also had a different personal Quran. He added two chapters called "*Sura Al-Hafd*" and "*Sura Al-Khal'*," and claimed that these were from the Quran (These "chapters" are still being recited by

	Hanefites in the "*sala* el witr," after night prayers.).
Following *hadith* books is equal to following the messenger.	Muhammad was given the Quran alone, and God alone issues the tenants of Islam (6:19, 38,114; 7:3; 12:111; 17:46; 31:6; 45:6; 69:38-47).

Hadith books were compiled from hearsay sources two centuries after Muhammad. One of the major sources of *hadith* is Jewish and Christian theology. Sunni and Shiite scholars have written volumes of books to identify and expose, though with little success, the piles of stories imported from the Jewish Mishna, Gemara and Old Testament, sources, which were called *Israiliyyat*. For instance, many Jewish stories and practices were imported to "Islam" via "convert" Jewish and Christian scholars, such as the concept of the Coming *Mahdi* (the Guiding Savior) and practice of circumcision, etc. Kab bin al Akhbar was one of those influential converts. Sunni scholars list Abdullah bin Abbas, Abu Hurayra, Abdullah bin Amr Ibnul As, Abdullah bin Salam, Tamim al-Dari, and Vahb bin Munabbih as the major narrators of *Israiliyyat*.

The *hadith* that should be the most authentic is the *hadith* about Muhammad's speech in *Hujjat al-Wada* (The Farewell Sermon) in which reportedly tens of thousands of his companions listened. The last statement of this sermon is reported in three different versions:

- I am leaving you the Quran and my *sunna*; you should follow both. (*Muwatta* 46/3).
- I am leaving you the Quran and my relatives; you should follow both. (*Muslim* 44/4/2408; *Ibn Hanbal* 4/366; *Darimi* 23/1/3319).
- I am leaving you the Quran; you should follow it. (Muslim 15/19/1218; Ibn *Majah* 25/84/3074; *Abu Dawud* 11/56/1905).

Another interesting *hadith* reported by *hadith* books speaks volumes:

"When Muhammad was sick on his death bed, he asked his companions to bring him pen and paper so that he could write them something for their salvation. When one of his companions rushed out to bring pen and paper, he was stopped by Omar Ben Khattab. Reportedly, Omar told him: "The prophet has a high fever; he does not know what he is saying. God's book is sufficient for us (*hasbuna kitabullah*!)" (*Bukhari*: Jihad 176, Jizya 6, Ilm 49, Marza 17, Magazi 83, Itisam 2; *Muslim*: Vasiyya 20-22; *Ibn Hanbal* 1/222, 324, 336, 355)

According to this "authentic" *hadith*, Muhammad dies without writing his last statement. The *hadith* above claims to be reporting

	the last words of prophet Muhammad and his companion's reaction. The alleged statements attributed to Omar Ben Khattab and acquiesced to by all other prominent companions shake and destroy the foundation of piles upon piles of *hadith*. In summary, *hadith* books contain many *hadith* rejecting *hadith* as a secondary source besides the Quran. They report the third version of the last statement in Muhammad's last sermon during pilgrimage, and they report the *hadith* about Omar not allowing any other writing from Muhammad since he and the other prominent companions thought God's book was sufficient for them. Yet despite these and many other "reported" negative remarks and prohibition about *hadith*, they collected thousands of them.
God gave Muhammad the Quran and other revelations *similar* to the Quran.	This claim is found in *hadith* books and is noteworthy that the Arabic text of the *hadith* uses exactly the same word, *mithl* (similar), thus defying God's challenge that the there is no book *similar* to the Quran (52:34). The books they consider *similar* to the Quran are ALL hearsay reports, filled with superstitions, contradictory claims, bad grammar, various dialects, trivial and frivolous rules, scientific inaccuracies, sectarian agendas, misogynistic ideas and practices, cruelty, tribal and racist ideologies, hero-worship, silly stories, and even commercials.
Calling oneself with the word Muslim alone is not sufficient. One must follow blindly (*taqleed*) a sect or order, such as Hanafi, Shafii, Hanbali, Maliki, Salafi, Naqshibendi, Jafari, Isna Ashari, Ahmadi, Qadiyani, Bahai, Nurcu, Rashadi, etc. We should follow the *fatwas* and *sharias* of *imams*, *mujtahids* and scholars of our sect without questioning. In other words we	God called us Muslims, that is, those who peacefully surrender themselves to God (22:78; 41:33). Dividing into sects and factions are among the attributes of polytheists (6:159; 23:52-56). Following parents, religious leaders, or anyone blindly is wrong and a source of evil (2:170; 5:104: 10:78,100; 17:36; 26:74; 31:21; 34:43; 43:22,23). The Quran warns us not to be hypnotized by the charisma of leaders, or by social conventions. A society comprised of individuals that value rational and empirical inquiry will never become the victim of religious fanaticism, tragedies brought by charismatic politicians and clergymen. A religion or sect that glorifies ignorance and gullibility can be very dangerous for its followers and others. As the Physicist Steven Weinberg once put profoundly, "With or without religion, you would have good people doing good things, and evil people doing evil things. But for good people to do evil things, that takes religion." (Steven Weinberg , *Facing Up : Science and Its Cultural Adversaries*, Harvard University Press, 2001, p. 242). We should add ideology to religion, since any dogmatic ideas can block rationality and turn humans to beasts. In the last century alone, communism and fascism inflicted too much pain on humanity.

must be *muqallids* (followers). Reason is not sufficient to find the truth. We need faith, and faith is superior to reason.	The Quran categorically rejects blind faith or credulity (17:36). The Islam described by the Quran is not a "religion" in the common sense of the word. Thus, we prefer calling Islam a system, rather than a religion. The word belief or faith is commonly used as a euphemism for wishful thinking or joining the bandwagon. Those who cannot justify their faith by deductive or inductive arguments, those who cannot provide compelling reason for why they believe certain dogmas and disbelieve others, are people who are not *muminun* (those who acknowledge) in accordance to the definition of the word by the Quran. If the author of the scripture is also the creator of the nature, and if it is He who is rewarding us with scientific knowledge and technology when we rationally and empirically investigate its laws, then why would He discourage us from using our mind and senses to investigate claims about Him and words attributed to Him? Otherwise, schizophrenia or inconsistency become divine attributes. God is not in the end of the dark tunnel of blind faith; but we can discover and get in touch with Him by tuning our mind and heart to get his message broadcast in the frequency of wisdom and knowledge. Therefore, according to the contextual semantics of the Quran, faith or belief denotes the conviction as a result of reason and compelling evidence. Thus, to distinguish the Quranic terminology of belief and faith from its common usage, we prefer the word "acknowledge."

This does not mean that a person who acknowledges the Quran will not have mysteries or unknowns. To the contrary. But, accepting mysteries and unknown should have compelling reasons. For instance, the idea of universe coming out of nothing, or an infinitely small and dense point called the singularity, the idea of Big Bang, is difficult to digest. We have no experience of such a thing. But, we have compelling evidence to accept Big Bang though we might have difficulty in comprehending it. Extraordinary claims require extraordinary evidence, and most religions do not even provide ordinary evidence for their extraordinary claims often riddled with contradictions and utter nonsense.

Abraham was a rational monotheist. Before his messengership, Abraham, as a young philosopher, reached the idea of the "greatest" by a series of hypothetical questions. His method of proving the existence of the creator of all things was both empirical and rational. He invited people to observe the heavenly bodies and then deduce the existence of an absolute creator from their contingent characteristics. This empirical and rational methodology is supported by God.

Abraham, not only supported his monotheistic faith through rational arguments, but also falsified the claims of his opponents via rational arguments by breaking the little statutes of his pagan people and sparing the biggest one. When the polytheists inquired about the "disbeliever/ingrate" who committed such a blasphemous act to their idols, Abraham stood up and pointed at the biggest statute, thereby forcing his people to reflect and examine their religious dogmas (21:51-67).

The Quran provides a rational argument for why God cannot have partners or equals. The argument in verse 21:21-22 is a logical argument called Denying Antecedent. Thus, it is no wonder that the Quran invites us not to be gullible. We should not follow anything without sufficient knowledge, including belief in God.

The Quran rejected the Christian metaphor of sheep and shepherd and instructed Muslims not to use any word that implies such subjugation (2:104). Despite the Quran's clear warnings against being a sheep in a flock, followers of *hadith* adopted the teachings of St. Paul and turned themselves to sheep, and rational monotheism into irrational polytheism.

The word *raina* (shepherd us) referred in verse 2:104 implies to be lead like sheep. Muslims do not and should not follow anyone, including prophets blindly, without using their intelligence, reasoning and senses. No wonder, obeying the leader is limited by the standard of *maruf*, that is known or knowledge (60:12). However, the Bible uses the shepherd/sheep analogy to depict the relationship between people and their leaders. "And I will set up one shepherd over them, and he shall feed them, even my servant David; he shall feed them, and he shall be their shepherd" (Ezekiel 34:23). Jesus Christ is likened to a good shepherd (John 10:14; Heb 13:20). Kings and leaders are too considered like shepherds (Isaiah 44:28; Jeremiah 6:3; 49:19). Ministers of the gospel too are likened to shepherds (Isaiah 56:11; Jeremiah 50:6; Jeremiah 23:4; Ezekiel 34:2,10). Also, see: Zechariah 10:2; Psalms 78:52; Psalms 119:176.

This metaphor would be abused to its full capacity by St. Paul, the dubious figure who distorted the monotheistic message of Jesus after his departure. St. Paul fabricated many stories and practices, including justification of receiving money for preaching. When the true followers of the *Injeel*, that is, the Good News, criticized him, he defended his "milking" the congregation by resorting to the Biblical metaphor, and twisting the original purpose of metaphor. See: 1 Corinthians 9:7.

The Biblical phrase, "Know the truth, and the truth will set you free!" (John 3:24), is a powerful statement against idolatry and ignorance. However, St. Paul and his followers turned the wisdom preached by Jesus into bigotry and dogmatism, which considered philosophy and philosophers the enemy. Millions of religious people, who are capable and smart human beings in the outside world, are so brainwashed by religious lies since their childhood, that they feel proud of being called sheep in their temples! Most

41

	faithful of religions nod positively at Voltaire's depiction of the level of their understanding: "The truths of religion are never so well understood as by those who have lost the power of reasoning." (Voltaire, Philosophical Dictionary, 1764) If you really want to name yourself with suffixes such as an –ist, –ite, or –an, then you should call yourself Truthist, Truthite, or Truthian! Or, you might just call yourself, Godist, Godite, Godian!
Some verses of the Quran abrogate/invalidate other verses of the Quran. For instance, 2:180 and 2:219 are invalid. Even some *hadith* abrogate verses of the Quran. For instance, a *hadith* adds another prohibition to 4:24 and thus abrogate its claim of exhaustive enumeration. Another example is that Muhammad forbade leaving a will for the relatives and thus abrogated the instruction of 4:23-24; 2:180, and 4:11-12.	There is no abrogation in the Quran (2:85; 4:82; 15:90-92; 12:110-111; 45:6). The blasphemous claim of abrogation is based on the distortion of the meaning of the word *ayat*, in singular form, in 2:106, and a lack of understanding of the context and connection of verses with each other. The idea of abrogation implies contradiction and rejection of the divinity of the Quran (4:82).
The Quran is not clear; it is ambiguous.	The Quran is clear and easy to understand for those who acknowledge the truth and use their God-given intelligence (5:15; 54:17,22,32,40; 11:1; 17:46; 18:57; 26:195).
The Quran is not detailed; it is general. For instance, the Quran does not inform us how to observe the	The Quran is sufficiently detailed by God the Most Wise, and it reminds us of this aspect repeatedly (6:19,38,55,97,114-116,119,126; 7:32,52,174; 9:11; 10:5,24,37; 11:1; 12:111; 13:2; 17:12; 30:28; 41:3; 41:44; 79:19). The Quran mentions *sala* prayer in about seventy verses and provides the details God deemed sufficient, not the trivial details

42

sala prayers.	demanded by people and fabricated by clergymen. *Hadith* books do not contain better words than the Quran, and they do not have additional video clips of Muhammad showing us how to pray. To the contrary, they contain various verbal hearsay accounts full of contradictions. For instance, according to some *hadith,* Muhammad did not recite anything else after reciting the first chapter of the Quran, contradicting other reports. Some *hadiths* report that Muhammad made ablution after touching his wife's hand, but you will find other *hadiths* on the next page denying that. Besides, no sane person would accept all the lies and harmful teachings of *hadith* and *sunna* for the sake of *sala* prayer. It is better not to observe *sala* prayer at all, which should lead to good deeds, than committing all the atrocities, ignorance, and idol-worship promoted by *hadith, sunna,* and *sharia.* The followers of *hadith* and *sunna,* for the sake of being able to perform a fabricated *sala* with numerous trivial details, have traded the message of the Quran with volumes of contradictory books. There cannot be a worse trade than this (10:15).
The Quran is not complete; it needs to be completed.	The Quran is God's word and it is complete (6:115; 19:64; 18:109). Asking trivial or irrelevant questions regarding practices and demanding more rules and instructions creates problems and confusion (2:67-70; 5:101).
The Quran alone does not guide; it needs many other books and teachings.	The Quran is sufficient to guide those who are appreciative and intelligent (5:48-49; 6:112-114,159; 7:3; 10:15; 17:39,45-46; 25:30; 31:6; 36:2; 39:23,38; 35:43).
The earth is standing on the horns of a giant bull.	That might explain why wearing red colored clothes is prohibited by *hadith and sunna!*

As we stated above these and many other religious instructions containing idol-worship, misogynistic attitudes and practices, superstitions, and numerous prohibitions that make life miserable for the religious people, replaced the message of the Quran. This was accomplished by claiming that the Quran is incomplete and lacks detail, by distorting several verses of the Quran, such as "obey God and his messenger," and by taking verses and even phrases out of their context, such as "whatever the messenger gives you take it, and whatever he enjoins you leave it." To prove their point, they fabricated countless *hadiths* containing frivolous details, such as how to enter bathrooms, how many stones

43

to use for cleaning yourself in the bathroom, how to hold one's hands or fingers during the prayers, how long one should grow his moustache and beard, what color is not proper for shirts, how to brush one's teeth, etc. When people did not find those frivolous or unnecessary details in the Quran, the propagandists of Sunni or Shiite religions would present them with *hadith* and sectarian jurisprudence as an explanation, complement, or supplement to the Quran. Thus, God's protected word was deemed to be in need of the unprotected lies and false claims fabricated by ignorant people. God's system was turned into a religion of limited partners.

Years ago, the Theology Faculty at the University of Istanbul held a panel discussion on "Understanding of Islam." The participants were prominent professors of theology. The professor of *fiqh* (sectarian jurisprudence) pontificated that the Quran could not be understood without studying and understanding the Sunni literature on *fiqh* and *usul ul- fiqh* (procedure of jurisprudence). The professor of mysticism softly argued that "the Quran could not be understood without studying and practicing mysticism." According to the professor of *hadith,* too "the Quran could not be understood without studying and understanding the *hadith* and its procedures." Finally, according to the professor of *Siyar*, history of Muhammad and his companions, "the Quran could not be understood without studying and understanding the history of the time."

All four participants of the panel were in agreement regarding how meaningless the Quran was. They even had a consensus on this. Their blind followers should just forget about studying the Quran, but they should start digging into hundreds of volumes of contradictory sectarian teachings. Instead of telling people that in order to understand *fiqh*, *hadith*, mysticism, and the history of Islam, in order to separate hay from grain, that they should first study and comprehend the Quran, they were arguing for a backward methodology. They were putting hundreds of volumes of contradictory mishmash literature between the individual and God's word. This led to the creation of a different discipline called the "the science of reconciling the contradictions among *hadiths*" where silly defenses developed to promote and maintain the authority of the fabrications. They knew well that none would be able to make it to the Quran, and even if they made it, they would be blind to perceive the light of the Quran through their filters, smoke and fog.

The Prophecy of the Quran Regarding
the Quadrinity of *Hadith*, *Sunna*, *Ijmah* and *Sharia*.

It is interesting that God informs us that Muhammad's only complaint will be about his people's desertion of the Quran (25:30). He will not complain that we deserted his *sunna*, as *hadith* books want us to believe. Those who are expecting their idol Muhammad to save them in the hereafter through his exclusive power of intercession will be surprised to witness rejection by their idols.

Knowing that ignorant and unappreciative people would ignore the Quran and would trade its enlightening and progressive message with the dark teachings of *hadith, sunna, ijma* and *sharia*, God uses these words in a prophetic way:

- It is noteworthy that the word *hadith* is always used in negative way when it is used to depict human utterances (12:111; 31:6; 33:53; 45:6; 52:34; 66:3).
- The Quran never uses the word *sunna* in connection with Muhammad. There is only one valid *sunna* (law, mould, example) and it is *sunnatullah* (God's law, mould, example), and God's *sunna* for previous generations is usually negative because of their corruption and aggression. (33:38,62; 35:43; 40:85; 48:23)
- Similarly, the Quran does not use the word *ijma* (consensus) in a positive sense when it is used to describe the actions of people (20:60; 70:18; 104:2; 3:173; 3:157;10:58; 43:32; 26:38; 12:15; 10:71; 20:64; 17:88; 22:73; 54:45; 28:78; 7:48; 26:39; 26:56; 54:44).
- Interestingly, the sectarian teaching that reflects the opinion of the idolized imams is called *sharia* (law; path) and it is too condemned when it refers to other than God's law (42:21). We must obey God's law (42:13; 5:48; 45:18).

Now let us get some details about the astonishing fulfillment of the Quranic prophecy regarding the first idol, *hadith*.

The following verses describe the early enemies of the truth during the era of Muhammad, but their message did not expire with the passage of time. To the contrary, the language of the verses is prophetic and it describes the misguided people of all times. Here are the prophetic verses informing us about the enemies of Prophet Muhammad who would fabricate lies called ***hadith***:

"And they swore by God using their strongest oaths; that if a sign came to them they would appreciate it. Say, 'The signs are from God.' For all you know, once it comes **they will not appreciate!**' We divert their hearts and eyesight, as they did not acknowledge it the first time; and We leave them wandering in their transgression. Even if We sent down to them the angels, even if the dead spoke to them, and if We had gathered before them everything, they still would not acknowledge except God wills it. But **most of them are ignorant**. We have permitted the enemies of every prophet, human and Jinn devils, to **inspire** in each other with **fancy *hadith*** in order to deceive. Had your Lord willed, they would not have done it. You shall disregard them and their **fabrications**. That is so the hearts of those who do not appreciate the Hereafter will listen to it, and they will accept it, and they will take of it what they will. 'Shall I seek **other than God as a judge** when He has sent down to you **this book sufficiently detailed**?' Those to whom We have given the book know that it is sent down from your Lord with truth; so do not be of those who have doubt. The **word of your Lord has been completed** with truth and justice; there is no changing His words. He is the Hearer, the Knower. If you obey the **majority** of those on Earth, they will lead you away from God's path; that is because **they follow conjecture**, and that is because they only guess. Your Lord is sufficiently aware of who strays from His path, and He is sufficiently aware of the guided ones." (6:109-116)

Knowing that the enemies of Jesus fabricated the doctrine of the Trinity and associated him as a partner with the One God by creating multiple personalities for God, similarly the so-called Muslims too fabricated *hadith* books and associated Muhammad as a partner with God in His judgment. The Quran informs us about many ways of setting partners with God, or polytheism. A careful reader will notice that the verses quoted above reject all the major excuses used by the proponents of *hadith* and *sunna*. These verses describe the followers of fancy *hadiths* with the following qualities:

- Despite their lip service, they do not appreciate God's signs. (We have witnessed a modern example of this ingrate reaction to the prophetic fulfillment of chapter 74).
- Most of them are ignorant, blind followers.
- They tell each other fancy *hadiths* presenting them as divine inspiration or revelation.
- The *hadiths* that they are narrating to each other are fabrications.
- Despite their lip service, they do not appreciate the hereafter.
- They seek Muhammad and other idols as partners with God's judgment regarding islam.
- They do not accept that the Quran is sufficiently detailed.
- They do not accept that God's word is complete.
- They put too much confidence in the numbers of those who follow their sect; they follow the crowd.
- They follow conjecture.

The Quran does not use the word "*hadith*" negatively in a haphazard manner. The language of the Quran and its choice of words is very precise. God knew that the idol worshipers would call those fabrications "*hadith*." It is interesting that they did not call their lies "*aqwal* = sayings," "*akhbar* = narrations," "*hikam* = aphorisms," "*athaar* = teaching/tradition" or any other word from the rich Arabic language. They unwittingly termed their inventions "*hadith*" (narrative, discourse, story, or recent event). This is a fulfillment of the Quranic projection. Whenever the Quran uses *hadith* for other than the Quran, it attaches a negative meaning to it. Since the followers of the fabricated narrations and hearsays are not translating the name of those fabrications into English or other languages, to expose the true nature of their teachings, and to unveil the clear Quranic connection, we will also keep the word *hadith* untranslated:

> 12:111 This is not a **fabricated** *hadith*. It is a confirmation of previous scriptures, **detailing everything**, and a **guide** and **mercy** for those who appreciate.

The followers of fabricated *hadiths* claim that the Quran is not sufficiently detailed! They thus reject God's repeated assertion that the Quran is "complete, perfect, and sufficiently detailed" (6:19,38,114), and thus justify the creation of volumes of *hadith*, and a library full of contradictory teachings that are supposed to complete the Quran. By reflecting on 12:111 above, one can see God's answer to those fabricators and their followers. God informs us that we do not need fabricated *hadith*; that the Quran as a sufficiently detailed guide, is all we need. The Quran is the only "*ahsan al-hadith*" (best statement) to be followed (39:23).

In 12:111, God the Most Wise, rejects both the "*hadith*" and the basic excuse for accepting it as a source of Islam. No excuse is accepted from the followers of *hadith* in this world, nor on the Day of Judgment. God asks them:

> 45:6 In which hadith, besides God and His revelations do they acknowledge?

They reply, "We believe in Bukhari, Muslim, Tirmizi, Ibn Hanbal, Kafi, Nahj-ul Balaga, and more besides God's revelations." God challenges the idol worshipers:

> 52:34 Let them produce a hadith like this, if they are truthful.

As a response, they slander the prophet in one of their holy *hadith* books:

> "The prophet, peace be upon him, said, 'I was given the Quran and a *hadith* like it'." (Abu Dawood)

Does the Quran use the word *hadith* in connection to Muhammad? Yes, the word *hadith* has been attributed to Muhammad twice. But, not in the way Sunnites and Shiites would hope. These two occurrences have clear implications. First, the Omniscient God uses them for the prophet's personal statements, not for his religious teachings, which is limited with the Quran alone. Second, in both occasions, God Almighty uses the word *hadith* with injunctions. Here are the verses:

> 33:53 . . . When you finish eating, you shall leave; without lingering to hadith (converse). . .

> 66:3 The prophet had confided some of his wives with a hadith (statement/story/event), then one of them spread it. . .

As you see in the verses above, when the word "*hadith*" is attributed to prophet Muhammad in the Quran, several interesting points are made. *Hadith* is the prophet's personal statements, and we should not seek them (33:53) and we should not transmit them to others (66:3). Unfortunately, those who did not respect the Quran and prophet Muhammad, fabricated many *hadiths* about Muhammad's private and sexual life with his wives. Ironically, they attributed the worst insults to Muhammad while they were declaring their love and allegiance to him.

(For an argument titled, "Why Trash All the *Hadith*?," see the Articles section of www.IslamicReform.org)

A Sample From *Hadith* Books:

Below is a sample from various *hadith* books, collections of hearsay and false teachings:

- "A group from the Uraynah and Uqaylah tribes came to the prophet and the prophet advised them to drink urine of camels. Later on, when they killed the prophet's shepherd, the prophet seized them, gouged out their eyes, cut their hands and legs, and left them thirsty in the desert" (Bukhari 56/152, Hanbal 3/107,163).
- "I am the most honorable messenger, on the day of the judgment only I will think of my people" (Bukhari 97/36).
- "Do not make any distinction among the messengers; I am not even better than Jonah" (Bukhari 65/4,5; Hanbal 1/205,242,440).
- "Bad luck is in the woman, the horse, and the home" (Bukhari 76/53).
- "If a monkey, a black dog or a woman passes in front of a praying person, his prayer is nullified" (Bukhari 8/102; Hanbal 4/86).
- The hell will be filled with mostly women; women are deficient in intelligence and religion (Muslim, Iman 34/132; Muslim, Iydayn 4; Tirmizi, Iman 6/2613; Ibn Majah, Fitan 19/4003; Ahmad b. Hanbal, Musnad, II/373-374, II/318; Abu Dawud, *Sunna* 15/4679; Nasai, Iydayn 19).
- "The prophet gave permission to kill children and women in war" (Bukhari, Jihad/146; Abu Dawud 113).
- "The earth is carried on a giant bull; when it shakes its head an earthquake occurs" (Ibn Kathir 2/29; 50/1).
- "Leaders have to be from the Quraish tribe" (Bukhari 3/129,183; 4/121; 86/31).
- "You shall kill all black dogs; because they are devils" (Hanbal 4/85; 5/54).
- "God is the time" (Muwatta 56/3).
- "To prove His identity, God opened his legs and showed the prophet His thigh" (Bukhari 97/24, 10/129 and the comment on the Sura 68).
- "The parchment that the verse about stoning to death for adultery was written on was eaten and abrogated by a goat" (Ibn Majah 36/1944; Ibn Hanbal 3/61; 5/131,132,183; 6/269).

- "A man from the tribe of Banu Aslam came to the Prophet and informed him that he had committed illegal sexual intercourse and he bore witness four times against himself. The Prophet ordered him to be stoned to death as he was married." (Bukhari, *hadith* 6814)
- "A tribe of monkeys arrested an adulterous monkey and stoned it to death, and I helped them" (Bukhari 63/27).
- "When the prophet died his armor had been pawned to a Jew for several pounds of barley" (Bukhari 34/14,33,88; Hanbal 1/ 300; 6/42,160,230).
- "The punishment for cutting the fingers of a woman is to pay her: 10 camels for one finger, 20 camels for two fingers, 30 camels for three fingers, and 20 (twenty) camels for four fingers" (Hanbal 2/182; Muvatta 43/11).
- "The prophet had been bewitched by a Jew, and for several days he did not know what he was doing" (Bukhari 59/11; 76/47; Hanbal 6/57; 4/367).
- "Muhammad possessed the sexual power of 30 men" (Bukhari).
- "Do not eat and drink with your left hand, because Satan eats and drinks with the left hand" (Hanbal 2/8,33).
- "The prophet eats odd number of dates on Id-ul-Fitr" (Bukhari 2/73).
- "The Prophet said, 'Whoever performs ablution should clean his nose with water by putting the water in it and then blowing it out, and whoever cleans his private parts with stones should do it with odd number of stones'" (Bukhari 1/162, 1/163).
- "The prophet said: 'Do not write anything from me except the Quran. Whoever wrote, must destroy it" (Muslim, Zuhd 72; Hanbal 3/12,21,39).
- "The prophet ordered Amr Ibn As to write everything that he speaks" (Hanbal 2/162).
- "Omar said: Quran is enough for us, do not write anything from the prophet. Everyone in the room accepted what Omar said." (Bukhari, Jihad 176, Jizya 6, Ilim 49, Marza 17, Magazi 83, Itisam 26; Muslim, Wasiyya 20,21,22).

A Sample From *Sharia* And *Fatwas* Of Scholars: Muhammad As Their Potty Trainer

While surfing the Internet, we encountered a *fatwa* from a renowned cleric who is falsely called *alim* (knowledgeable person). The field of his expertise, his audience, the extent of his "knowledge," the relevancy of the information to human life, the number of citations from *hadith* books, his ignorance of the Quran, and his blind followers, all provide many reasons why Sunnis and Shiites are in such miserable shape in the contemporary world. Those who think they need holy *hadiths* as a manual on how to go to the bathroom, those who think that potty-training adults was among one of the many missions of prophet Muhammad, those who follow these and many more frivolous rules, will not have brains left to deal with "more important issues." The Saudi cleric, Sheikh Muhammad Saleh Al-munajjid, who derived 13 holy rules for bathroom etiquette from *hadith* books, leaves no hope for cure with his closing statement (For the entire *fatwa*, visit www.islamicreform.org). Instead of being embarrassed about his indulgence in odd bathroom manners and odd numbers of stones, he shows the audacity to brag about these silly instructions:

> "If the Shari`ah has paid such minute attention to the details of such a mundane matter, what do you think it has to say about more important issues? Do you know of any other religion or system in the world that has brought laws like these? This is enough, by Allah, to prove its perfection and beauty, and the necessity of following it."

If this is an example and beauty of *Sharia* about minute issues, may Allah save humanity from its verdict on important issues! We do not know how many so-called Muslims feel guilty for not being able to follow all these rules. We do not know how many Sunnis urinated in their pants while trying to follow all these holy bathroom rules. Though this particular cleric generously interpreted the *hadith* to save his flock from this hassle in buildings, we do not know how many scrupulous followers sit backward on the bathroom seats in order not to face *qibla* (direction of *Kaba*), or how many of them employ high tech gadgets such as GPS made by the "infidels" to find their direction in the bathrooms. However, we know for sure, that any group of people following these and many other piles and piles of fabricated rules have lost their chance for progress and prosperity. No wonder, the Quran reminds us of the importance of reasoning and the importance of staying away from religious clerics who make up *sharia* in the name of God:

> "No person may acknowledge except by God's leave. And He afflicts the filth upon those who do not reason." (10:100)

> "Or do they have partners who decree for them a law (*sharia*) which has not been authorized by God? And if it were not for the word already given, they would have been judged immediately. Indeed, the transgressors will have a painful retribution." (42:21)

Abusing the verses of the Quran

Many verses of the Quran have been distorted or taken out of context to promote the volumes of hearsay fabrication. Here are the most frequently abused Quranic verses:

- The Quran instructs us to follow the messenger (4:59); so we must follow Bukhari, Muslim, Tirmizi, Ibn Hanbal, Ibn Maja, Abu Dawud, Kafi, Nahj al-Balaga, and many other books.

- The Quran informs us that the messenger explains the Quran (16:44); so we must follow Bukhari, Muslim, Tirmizi, Ibn Hanbal, Ibn Maja, Abu Dawud, Kafi, Nahj al-Balaga, and many other books.
- The Quran informs us that the messenger does not speak on his own (53:3-4); so we must follow Bukhari, Muslim, Tirmizi, Ibn Hanbal, Ibn Maja, Abu Dawud, Kafi, Nahj al-Balaga, and many other books.
- The Quran advises us to take whatever the messenger gives us and abstain from what he forbid us (59:7); so we must follow Bukhari, Muslim, Tirmizi, Ibn Hanbal, Ibn Maja, Abu Dawud, Kafi, Nahj al-Balaga, and many other books.
- The Quran warns us not to put our opinion before that of the messenger (49:1). Thus, we must follow Bukhari, Muslim, Tirmizi, Ibn Hanbal, Ibn Maja, Abu Dawud, Kafi, Nahj al-Balaga, and many other books.
- The Quran tells us that there is a good example in the messenger of God (33:21), so we must follow Bukhari, Muslim, Tirmizi, Ibn Hanbal, Ibn Maja, Abu Dawud, Kafi, Nahj al-Balaga, and many other books.

A careful reader of the Quran would notice that the verses referred to above were subjected to a cunning distortion and abuse to transform Muhammad from being the deliverer of God's message, from being a mailman of God, to another authority besides God, to God's partner in authoring God's system. Not only did they turn the system of Islam into peacefully surrendering to a religion designed by multiple partners, they also promoted various hearsay sources collected centuries after Muhammad, according to their sectarian and tribal preferences.

Here, as an example, we will discuss briefly one of the oft-quoted verses, "A good example has been set for you by the messenger of God" (33:21). Those who wish to produce volumes of *hadith* books out of this verse ignore the fact that a similar statement is also made about Abraham: "A good example has been set for you by Abraham and those with him" (60:4, 6). If verse 33:21 requires Muhammad's *hadith*, then why would not the verses 60:4,6 require Abraham's *hadith*? Which books narrate *hadiths* from Abraham? Obviously, the only reliable source for both examples is the Book of God, which narrates the relevant exemplary actions. It also warns us not to repeat the mistakes committed by Muhammad (33:37; 80: 1-10).

Let us briefly discuss the second example to see better the nature of abuse, and how thousands of *hadith* rabbits are produced from empty hats. One of the most frequently cited Quranic instructions is "obey God and His Messenger" (4:59). Obeying Bukhari, a narrator of hearsay, is not obeying the messenger. Obeying the messenger is obeying the complete, perfect and fully detailed Quran. Verse 25:73 describes the attitude of truth-seekers towards God's revelations. But the followers of *hadith* and *sunna* are very good in ignoring them. They do not see 6:19, 7:3, and 50:45, which say that the only teaching delivered by God's messenger was the Quran. They do not think that Muhammad practiced the

51

Quran, and the Quran alone (5:48, 49). They do not hear Muhammad's only complaint about his people (25:30). They do not understand that Muhammad disowns those who do not understand that the Quran is enough and fully detailed (6:114). The first verse of Chapter 9 states that an ultimatum is issued from God and His messenger. Muslims acknowledge that verses about the ultimatum are entirely from God. God did not consult Muhammad about the ultimatum. Muhammad's only mission was to deliver God's message (16:35; 24:54). Thus, the reason that God included the messenger in 9:1 is not because he was another authority in issuing it, but because he participated as the deliverer of the ultimatum. Similarly, because people receive God's message through messengers, we are ordered to obey the messengers. We also know that the Quran is a permanent messenger (65:11), and the Quran is a reminder and deliverer of good news (41:4; 11:2).

In Which Flavor and Shape do You Want Your Muhammad to be?

The falsifiers have presented a concoction of medieval Arab, Pagan, Jewish and Christian culture as good examples of the messenger. However, if you look at the context of the verse 33:21, the good example has been described as the messenger's courage and his constant remembrance of God. They extended this good example to irrelevant individual or cultural behaviors. For instance, they sanctified the beard and turban, ignoring the fact that the Meccan idol worshipers, such as Amr bin Hisham (aka, Abu Jahl) and Walid b. Mugiyra also had long beards and big turbans.

What is worse, the actions and words ascribed to prophet Muhammad have depicted him with a character that is far from exemplary. The *hadith* books portray the prophet as a phantasmagoric character with multiple personalities. That character is more fictitious than mythological gods and goddesses, such as Hermes, Pan, Poseidon and Aphrodite. He is a pendulous character, both bouncing up to deity, and down to the lowest degree. He is both wise and moronic. He is sometimes more merciful than God and sometimes a cruel torturer. He is both perfect and criminal, humble and arrogant, chaste and a sex maniac, trustworthy and a cheater, illiterate and educated, rich and poor, a nepotistic and a democratic leader, caring and a male chauvinist, an acknowledger and an ingrate, prohibiting *hadith* and promoting *hadith*. You find numerous conflicting personalities presented as an exemplary figure. Choose whichever composite character you like out of thousands of different examples. Those with preconceived ideas may go fish out *hadith* to support any personality or role model they want to carve out of the hero called Muhammad. Want a terrorist? You will find a few *hadiths* to justify it. He did after all, according to Bukhari, justify killing women and children in battle. Want a lamb? You will again find a few *hadiths* to depict him that way. When the children of Taif stoned him, he prayed for them. *Hadith* books contain almost anything you wish, especially about Muhammad. You may find an extremely kind and nice Muhammad besides a cruel torturer one. You may find Muhammad to be a

52

person with great morals on one page and on another page, you will see him a pedophile. You will find Muhammad pointing at the moon and splitting it into two pieces letting one piece fall into Ali's backyard, and on another page, you will find a Muhammad incapable of reading a simple letter.

Hadith books, by their very nature, are perfect sources for such abuse. They contain fragments of hearsay that were produced within several centuries with multiple authors, numerous agendas, inconsistent language/terminology, unreliable and fragmented contexts, and divisible or severally liable authorities. An "expert" can subject almost any *hadith* he dislikes to one of the rules of procedure called *usul ul-hadith* with multiple standards. The evaluation of the narrator by using another hearsay, partisanship, tribalism, racism, or personal scrupulousness, is called "*jarh*" and "*tadeel*" simply meaning, "trash" and "save." For instance, the most prominent Sunni *hadith* collector Bukhari who grew up in Bukhara, collected *hadiths* two hundred or so years after the departure of Muhammad. This story collector, while bragging about how meticulous he was, claims that he once traveled for about a month to hear a particular *hadith* from a narrator. When he visited him, he saw him deceiving his horse to the barn with an empty bag. Consequently, our meticulous Bukhari gave up from collecting the story he was going to report! In other words, he used the tool of "*jarh*" (trash) to cross over that particular narrator. Looking at the quality of the 7275 *hadiths* he allegedly picked out of 600,000 reported *hadiths* (99% defective material!), we can easily infer that he was not very lucky or did not have very good eyes in witnessing thousands of more deceivers with their horses. Ironically, this Bukhari narrates *hadith* from drunkard and oppressive Umayyad governors, and hundreds of *hadith* from Abu Hurayra who according to Bukhari himself was considered a congenial liar and fabricator by his prominent peers such as Omar, Ibn Abbas and Aisha. Either Bukhari was himself a deceived horse or another deceiver.

Let's sidetrack here and do a simple calculation. Bukhari, in his introduction, uses a first-class sales pitch according to the standards of the medieval era. He, or the later editors and promoters of his collection, try hard to depict the portrait of a devout, genius, scrupulous, and steadfast scholar. Although his Christian counterpart, St. Paul, was more articulate and more cunning in his self-promotion, history is a witness to the fact that Bukhari has done a similarly good job in another market. In the introduction of the collection called Bukhari, we learn that this celebrated *hadith* collector endured long trips, occasionally from one country to another, just to collect one *hadith*. We also learn that he was very careful in his evaluation of the chain of narrators; he was so pious that he performed ablution and prayed before recording each of his *hadith*s. We might be surprised to see, in the same section of this solemn promotional introduction, some funny animated clips too. For instance, we learn that some of the prophet's companions witnessed a group of monkeys stoning an adulterer monkey in the jungle (perhaps that provided some inspiration and imagination for later *hadith*s narrations involving the story of the holy hungry goat). Well, let's do some calculations...Let's assume that Bukhari told us the truth regarding the 600,000 *hadith*s he listened to and evaluated. Let's also be extremely generous to Bukhari and assume that on average it took him only one hour to go, interview, and evaluate each of the 600,000 *hadith*s, 99% of which he would later trash. Let's assume that he started wandering around, seeking *hadith* narrators, listening to them, and evaluating the chain of narrators from dawn until dusk. Let's assume that all his days were summer days, so that he worked ten hours a day without a break. Since we do not have any claim by Bukhari or another "holy" person regarding Bukhari's ability to inflate time, create time within time, or slow down time, we assume he worked like a super human being limited by the natural law. With these assumptions, Bukhari who lived 60 years, between 810-870 AC, would need 60,000 days, or 164 years. In other words, he would need more than a hundred years to be able to do what he was bragging about.

Yes, this Bukhari and his ilk have hijacked Muhammad, and have replaced the light of the Quran, with the darkness of ignorance.

Arabic fancy jargon are frequently used to impress non-Arabs to overwhelm them into believing that the "experts" indeed have an incredible amount of special knowledge; perhaps specially granted by God. The "expert" might evaluate the trustworthiness of one of the narrators listed in the chain, by various contradictory rules already established by previous *hadith* scholars. The *hadith* can then be classified in one of the numerous ranks of authenticity and thus discarded in favor of another one. Only a handful *hadith*s, which are called *mutawatir* (allegedly narrated by many people), may escape ending up in the trash via an arbitrary scrutiny of a determined scholar. Ironically, there is not even a consensus on the *mutawatir hadith*s. They do not call it "trash can" but they have invented fancy names to label how deep and stinky their cans are, labeling them *mursal, hasan, daif, mawdu*, etc. If you are a *muqallid*, that is a blind follower of a particular sect or order, then you pick what they have already picked for you. Your choice might be more limited with the leftover *hadith*s evaluated by the scholars, but you can be sure that by even staying as a *muqallid* in a particular sect, you will find plenty of room for wiggling around to make up your own religion. But, you can be sure that your choices will be limited to medieval Arab, Jewish and Christian cultures. If you are living in a modern metropolitan city, you may not be able to escape developing multiple personalities separated from each other by two millennia.

Considering that most of the *hadith* narrations are *ahad*, that is allegedly narrated by only one person from Muhammad, their authenticity can always be challenged by how you may personally deem the chain of narrators and the *hadith* books. This provides many opportunities to hatch and mutate numerous custom-made religions, sects, sub-sects, orders, or sub-orders out of the mishmash collection of medieval culture. This peculiar aspect of *hadith* collection is well described by the prophetic verses of the Quran:

"Shall we treat the muslims (peaceful submitters/surrenderers) like the criminals? What is wrong with your judgment? Do you have a book where you can find anything you wish?" (68:35-38).

Unappreciative and Arrogant people Do Not Have Access to the Quran

The Quran is a miraculous book. The author of the Quran has put a barrier between the Quran and those who dogmatically and fanatically consider it insufficient for salvation (17:45; 18:57). It is ironic and curious that those who claim that the Quran is difficult to understand do not understand the very verses about the understanding of the Quran. Verses 7:3; 17:46; 41:44; 56:79 are extraordinary works of linguistic art containing both the thesis and its proof simultaneously, since their multiple-meaning language contains a guide to understand the Quran and an excuse for not understanding the Quran. Those who understand the language of these verses experience the fulfillment of a miracle when they witness people unable to understand and glorify their lack of understanding the very verses that condemn those who lack understanding.

You will find on the cover of almost all published Quranic manuscripts a few verses. If you check, you will probably find 56:77-79 written in Arabic calligraphy.

> 56:77-79 It is an honorable Quran. In a protected record. None can grasp it except those pure.

Why among hundreds of verses describing the Quran, did the convention decided on these verses? Out of more than 50 descriptive noun-adjectives used for the Quran, why would they pick "*Karym*" (Honorable)? *Al-Quran il-Karym*? Why not the more frequently used words such as *Zikr* (Message), *Hakym* (Wise), *Mubyn* (Clear), *Nur* (Light)? Why is this verse highlighted in connection to the Quran? Why are the verses repeatedly reminding us of the easy-to-understand language of the Quran not highlighted (54:17,22,32,40)? Or, why not one of these verses 12:111; 15:1; 17:9; 17:88; 17:89; 30:58; 41:3; 55:2?

We have all the reasons to suspect the intention of those who dedicated Chapter 36 (Ya Sin) to be recited in funerals for the DEAD, the chapter that contains the only verse declaring that the Quran is sent to remind the LIVING beings (36:70)! We have all the reasons to suspect the intention of those who picked the name *hadith*, a negative word when used for hearsay narrations and teachings other than the Quran, to depict another source besides the Quran! So, why did they pick the word "*Karym*" as the most common adjective for the Quran and verses 56:77-79 as the most common subtitle for the covers of manuscripts?

Those who appreciate the Quran know the answer of the question very well: The polytheistic clergymen and scholars who betrayed the Quran, reached a consensus in not understanding or misunderstanding 56:77-79, and they thought they could repel others from the Quran according to their misunderstanding. They distorted the meaning of these verses by claiming that those who do not have ablution, including the women who they considered "dirty" because of menstruation, "should not touch" the Quran. Now we may infer why the verse whose meaning has been distorted by consensus is picked for the cover of the Quran manuscripts. Now we may infer why the adjective mentioned in that verse was made the most popular adjective of the Quran. We think that this is a part of a diabolic conspiracy to prevent the Quran from becoming a pocket book, a book of quick reference; they keep the Quran on high shelves or nail it on high walls far away from the reach of people. Unfortunately, this plan has worked successfully. The Quran has been transformed from being a guide, a reference book, a map, a compass, into a dangerous object, a runaway train, a high-voltage transformer station! When the Quran becomes a book too-difficult-to-understand, impossible to ascertain its "high" meanings, and dangerous to touch, then rush in volumes of *hadiths*, loads of *sunna*, barrels of hearsay, mishmash heaps of sectarian teachings, piles of nonsense, tons of superstitions, hordes of holy men, and troops of holy merchants. This explains the misery, backwardness, oppression, repression, division, and corruption rampant in the so-called "Muslim countries."

The religion that "Muslims" inherited from their parents and try hard to practice today, has little to do with the system of peacefully surrendering to God alone, which was delivered by Muhammad through the Quran. These clergymen who arrogated themselves and falsely claimed to be the "*ulama*" (people of knowledge), polluted the message of Islam with ignorance. They fabricated numerous *sharias* (laws), prohibitions, veils, beards, turbans, rules for how to clean one's bottom, rules on how to pee in the bathroom, toothbrushes, right hands, left hands, right feet, left feet, *hadiths*, *sunnas*, intercession, holy hair, holy cloths, holy teeth, holy feet traces, *hazrats*, lords, saints, *mawlas*, *mahdis*, innocent *imams*, orders, sects, rosaries, amulets, dreams, holy loopholes, prayer caps, circumcisions, shrines, extra prayers, extra prohibitions, and numerous Arabic jargon such as *mandup, mustahap, makruh, sharif, sayyid* and more nonsense. Thus, the religion of Sunnis and Shiites contradict the divine laws in nature and scripture, and condemns its sincere followers to misery and backwardness. The religious leaders and their political allies contribute greatly to the backwardness of the Muslim world. In 1974 our Lord, the Almighty and Wise Creator, fulfilled a great prophecy starting a new era in the realm of theology that aims to reform us and open the path of progress with "one of the greatest" (74:30-37).

The majority of Sunnis and Shiites, hypnotized by their religious leaders, are unaware that the religion they are so passionately trying to follow is no different than the religion which was so passionately upheld by Abu Jahl (the father of ignorance) and Abu Lahab (the father of furious fire) during Muhammad's era. However, the message of the Quran is again shining and removing the darkness of ignorance and polytheism.

Witnessing that their spider webs and walls of ignorance are at risk, the professional religious men and their blind followers might create loud noise and stir clouds of dust. They might do everything in their power to prevent the masses from reading this translation and the arguments contained in it. They might use all kinds of slander, insults, false accusations, threats, and noise to prevent people from hearing its message.

Their effort will be in vain for the universal light of the Quran is shining again with all its wonders. Neither the borders of states nor the judges and laws of oppressive regimes can prevent this light; neither the *fatwas* of those with the mentality of the Inquisition, nor the plots and bloody wars of crusaders. The Islamic reform, by God's will, will occur and the system will once again be dedicated to God alone. Praise be to God.

> 54:17   And We made the Quran easy to learn. Do any of you wish to learn?

An Invitation to Jews, Christians, Muslims, and All

In this foreword, we focused on the incredible amount of distortions made in the message delivered by Muhammad. Christianity and Judaism are no different. Today's Christianity, with its dogmas and practices, is far way from the monotheistic teachings of Jesus, the son of Mary.

If Moses, Jesus, and Muhammad were back today, Jews would condemn the first as Anti-Semite, Christians would denounce the second as Anti-Christ, and Muslims would revile the third as the Dajjal (The imposter).

Imagine a religion that its members worship the murder weapon, perform rituals to pretend that they are drinking the blood and flesh of their heroic victim, claim that 1+1+1 equals to 1, adopt a word as their name which was used by none of the early followers, misspell and mispronounce the name of their hero, follow someone's teaching who was prophetically condemned by their hero, accept a formula that was coined by a self-appointed commission 325 years after the founder, sing love and peace yet be responsible for most of the blood-shed and weaponry in the world, mobilize even children for centuries of barbarism called Crusades, sell parcels of heaven, excommunicate scientists, burn the first translator of their holy book, burn women in witch-hunt craze, invent ingenious torture devises and torture many in their holy courts, declare the earth as the flat center of the world for more than a millennium, lead and pray for colonialists, defend and practice slavery and racism until the cause was lost, mostly side with kings and the wealthy, deny women from many of their rights, condemn the theory of evolution, support occupations and wars with jingoistic slogans... Yes, how can such a religion, with a fake name, with a fabricated doctrine, with bizarre pagan practices, and with such a miserable historical record and bitter fruits belong to God? How can it be attributed to a philosopher, to a peacemaker, to an advocate of the rights of the weak, to a human messenger of God? (For a more detailed critical evaluation of modern Christianity, see 19 Questions For Christians, by Edip Yüksel)

Idolization of human beings is the epidemic of all religions, and it is the most common tragedy of human history. According to the original teachings of all God's messengers, idol worship or setting up partners to God, is the biggest offense against God. Besides, the idolization of prophets, messengers, saints and the faith of human intercession creates religious abuse, oppression, conflict and fighting between children of Adam, who are servants of God.

When believers start idolizing their previous religious leaders, they develop the tendency to idolize their living religious leaders too. Instead of seeking the truth, they are attracted to names and titles. The clergymen, in order to take advantage of that weakness and gain more power over their subjects, focus their preaching on praising the departed heroes, instead of God.

These clergymen and their fanatic followers killed many people, destroyed many homes in the name of their incarnated gods. They fabricated many rules and prohibitions in the name of God, and with such a complicated religion, they secured their jobs as professional holy men. They made money and fame in the name of those human gods. And they claimed to have the power of intercession in their names--so much so that they sold keys to the heavens, turned temples and churches to big businesses.

If we want to follow the basic principles common among the Old, the New and the Final Testaments, if we want to stop religious exploitations, if we don't want to use our God-given reasoning faculties to its maximum capacity, if we want the unity of all the the monotheists of all religions, freedom for everyone, including for non-religious people, and if we want to attain eternal salvation, we must start a "Copernican revolution" in theology. Instead of Krishna-centered, Jesus-centered, Mohammed-centered religions, we must turn to the original center, to the God-centered model. To achieve this revolution, each of us must start questioning the formulas and teachings that have created gods out of humans like us.

In a time where religious fanatics are pushing the world for another Crusade or Holy War, in a time where the words Messiah, Rapture, Armageddon, Mahdi invite hostile masses to shed more and more of each other's blood, in a time when those in power and in positions of making profit from curtailing civil liberties, in a time when wars and occupations are playing on jingoistic and religious emotions, yes in such a time, people of intelligence and good intentions should come together and plant the seeds of tolerance, peace, reason, human rights, and unity of humanity.

On Israel, Palestine, Suicide Bombers, and Terror

Compared to their small population, the Jewish influence is immense in the global arena, financially, politically and culturally. Disproportionate to their population, Jews have exhibited astonishing examples in both good and bad, in both success and blunder, and they have enjoyed vivid presence in world politics for millenniums. This explains why the Quran mentions them so frequently. Well, may be it is also true the other way around.

After being subjected to genocide and atrocious tortures by fascist forces, Jews were scattered around the world as immigrants. Yet, they did not disappear from the global scene or take centuries to recover, as many other nations would do. Not surprisingly, with the help of major powers of the time they were able to establish their own independent state in 1948, soon after their almost utter annihilation; a state not in Germany, but in their historical land, which has once again become the focal point of a global conflict; stirring the world by showcasing human aggression, greed, hatred, cruelty, racism, and terror.

As it seems, victim nations too might repeat the crimes of their predators. One would expect Israel to be the first against racism and colonialism, yet Israel was the last government to cut its relationship with the racist apartheid regime in South Africa, reflecting the depth of its racist policy against Palestinians. One would expect Israel to be the first nation against the weapons industry, yet Israel is one of top weapon manufacturers and exporters in the world. The racist and colonial policy of Israel by no means should be generalized to all Jews. There are more Jews in the world who condemn this policy then those who perpetrate it, and many are ashamed of what is being done in their name. While we should condemn terrorism as a method to get back one's land and independence, we should also mention that there are many Arabs who are hoping for a just solution and peaceful co-existence with their Jewish cousins.

Jews and Muslims lived together in peace for centuries, and their current conflict is partially due to the early terrorist tactics used by Zionist guerillas, and partially due to a myriad of external forces who are trying to keep the fires burning. These external forces include the ambitions of UK-Inc and USA-Inc, the racist Zionist zealots, corrupt Mullahs, racist Sunni and Shiite zealots, Evangelical Crusaders, Weapon and Oil industries, who make massive amounts of money from the tension in the region. Unfortunately, super powers who mediated the negotiations have not honestly sought justice in this conflict. Perhaps, they deliberately wanted a continuous, yet controlled conflict in the region so that they could exploit its rich resources through puppet regimes.

In their pre-emptive war in 1967, the Israeli soldiers carried the verse 2:249 of the Quran over their tanks when they entered Sinai after defeating the Arabs, and their misguided Arab nationalism. Ironically, the evildoers among them pushed for further land-grab in the East, thereby subjecting Palestinian natives to racial discrimination, dislocation, humiliation, massacres, destruction of property/infrastructure, legalized torture, and assassinations. Israel deliberately did not set a border, rather it kept its borders flexible seeking excuses and occasionally provoking its dehumanized subjects so that it could invade new territories and create more settlements. Decades of suffering under the brutal and humiliating fascist occupation destroyed the hopes and aspiration of a Palestinian population and it gave birth to suicide bombers, which in turn provided more excuses for the occupational force to continue its invasion and barbarism. The West's propaganda machine distorts the real picture of the conflict and deceives Christendom by depicting the victimized Palestinians as the aggressor. The numbers speak clearly. The number of Palestinian civilians and children killed by Israeli occupying forces far greater than the number of Israeli civilians and children killed by suicide bombers. Palestinians gave up continuing a hopeless fight with slings and rocks against tanks. The world's indifference against injustice in the region, and on top of that, the support of the super powers of the brutal racist occupation, gave birth to global resentment and hatred among Muslims, triggering a global gang-terrorism challenging the legalized and glorified state-terrorism.

Islam (more accurately, Hislam) has been around for centuries, and compared to other religious groups Muslims do not fare more violent. An objective study of suicide terrorism will inform us that it has more to do with brutal occupations than religions or ideologies. Religion and ideologies are mostly used for justification and propaganda of the political cause. Robert Pape, of the University of Chicago, in his book Dying to Win: The Logic of Suicide Terrorism, rightly argues that suicide terrorism is not driven by religion but by occupations. He provides many examples, such as the suicide attacks of Marxist Tamil Tigers organization in Sri Lanka in 1990's that inspired Palestinians who were using slings, rocks and rifles against occupying Israeli soldiers and tanks before the Intifada of 2000. In fact, a great majority of suicide-terrorist campaigns carried out in Lebanon, Sri Lanka, Chechnya, Kashmir, and Palestine aimed to compel occupation forces to withdraw. No wonder, Ayman al-Zawahiri and his terrorist organization Islamic Jihad was born after Israel's occupation during the 1967 pre-emptive war. No wonder, Russian invasion and occupation of Afghanistan, together with the legalized US occupation of Middle East through puppet and oppressive kings and emirs gave birth to Osama bin Laden and al-Qaida. No wonder, Russian brutal occupation of Chechnya gave birth to Shamil Basayev and his terrorist organization. Again, it is no wonder that US occupation of Iraq gave birth to Abu Musab al-Zarqawi and hundreds of other suicide bombers. Though compared to rebels or insurgents, occupiers commit much worse acts of barbarism and terrorism on the population of lands they occupy, that state terrorism is cleverly hidden from the world. Ironically, occupiers who create these terrorist insurgents or contribute substantially to their growth, use the terrorist attacks to justify and continue their occupation. Occupying forces cleverly use fear, xenophobia, and patriotic emotions of the taxpayers and take advantage of their ignorance about foreign affairs. Government agencies work cleverly to depict their brutal and bloody occupation as a justified act against evil and barbarism. Secret agencies are showered with money to stage covert operations, flood the world with misinformation and disinformation campaigns. Talking heads in media and academics are secretly hired to promote the policy of occupations. No wonder, despite all the obvious fraud, deception, and lies, the mainstream American media gave green card to the Neocon-Zionist-Crusader coalition to justify their pre-emptive war against Iraq. The pictures of Rumsfeld shaking hands with Saddam at the time Saddam was committing his horrendous atrocities against Kurds and Iran as a puppet of US-Inc, somehow became a footnote, rather than an incriminating headline, demonstrating the hypocrisy of warmongers.

The cycle of violence has since been accelerated by religious fanatics on all sides. The Zionist-Crusader-Capitalist coalition on one side, and the Salafi-Mullah-Taliban coalition on the other side, each adding more fuel to the fire. Each with their own agendas. Zionists hope to grab more land, Crusaders pray for a bloody Armageddon followed by Rapture, the capitalist salivates for more profit from wars; and the other gang weep for the Mahdi to come with its sword to seek out Jews hiding behind rocks. Another aspect of recent conflict between Christendom and Muslims is the empty shoes of "evil" after the demise of communism. Global oligarchs, who strengthen their political and financial capital during conflicts and mass paranoia, were looking for a substitute to communism. With a mixture of covert operations, provocations, unjustified wars, tyrant puppets, the lesser-of-two-evil policy, and training future terrorists, the mission is almost accomplished.

Now, Muslims in general, and Arabs in particular will be christened as the new face of evil. Knowing the history, we should not be surprised to witness another genocide and another use of nuclear weapons, followed by tears of regret, confession sessions, and cry of "Never again!" So long as people do not use their God-given reasoning and follow their clergymen and politicians blindly, Satan will use every tool at his disposal to create artificial divisions, hostility and hatred among the children of Adam. And Satan, who has a successful record of enticing since Cain & Abel, has always found religious clergymen and jingoistic politicians to be his best allies in his acts of corruption, destruction, and bloodshed on earth.

To the East, Muslims, and the Middle East

The following words are not from an enemy of yours, but from someone who shares the same book and the same history. These are the words of someone who cares a great deal about you. Someone who cries at night for your plight, for the tragedies which have befallen you. This is someone who knows your generosity, your sincerity, your unfulfilled dreams, your aspirations, your tragedies, your fears, your follies and delusions. You should listen, at least once. Enough prejudice and bigotry. Enough paranoia and hatred.

We must acknowledge the truth so that the truth will set us free.

Before looking around to point fingers at the cause of your problems, first look at the mirror. I do not mean that you should ignore the imperialistic ambitions of other nations and their open or clandestine interferences with the politics, economy and culture of your people. But, you cannot change your condition unless you change yourself. You cannot glorify the invasions, aggressions, massacres, and imperialistic policy of corrupt Umayyad, Abbasid, and Ottoman caliphs in your history and at the same time morally be critical of others for doing the same. Had God given you the same superiority, perhaps you would inflict the earth with more corruption and destruction than your current powerful enemies. You cannot kick them out from your home unless you reform yourself and your home. You cannot demand mercy from others if you do not have mercy on yourself.

We must acknowledge the truth so that the truth will set us free from self-righteousness.

Go check the list of patents issued last year. Check and see how many of them belong to a group, nation, religion you identify with. It should tell you a lot you a lot about your position in a world where information and technological progress is so crucial. Go check the list of prosperous countries. Check see how many of them belong to a group, nation, religion you identify with. Centuries ago, you were a role model for civilization, justice, democracy, and freedom; once you were a pioneer in mathematics, astronomy, medicine, and philosophy. Now look around and look at the mirror; who are you? You followed the religious *fatwa* of a *sheikh ul-islam* (highest cleric within the Ottoman Empire) who prohibited the use of printing machine from 1455 to 1727 for 272 years, for 100,000 precious days, in a vast land stretching from North Africa to Iran, from today's Turkey to Arabian Peninsula. While Europe indulged in learning God's signs in nature, shared the knowledge via printing machines, and was rewarded by God with renaissance, reform, technology, and prosperity; you devolved and sunk further in your ignorance. While Europeans engaged in philosophical arguments, you recited the holy book no better than a parrot, the book that highlighted the importance of learning, questioning, discovery, and pursuit of knowledge. You marveled at handwritten books of hearsay and superstition, at the lousy arguments developed by Gazzali who with the full support of a king aimed to banish philosophy. While Europe sought for a better system to save themselves from the tyranny of kings and church, you recited handwritten poems to praise your corrupt kings and idols. No wonder why, your land, your name, your face, your religion is now associated with backwardness, ignorance, oppression, violence, and poverty. You have become the bum of the world.

We must acknowledge the truth so that the truth will set us free from our ignorance.

Once the religious among you hoped that the theocracy of mullahs would fulfill your dream, would bring back the glorious days of your past. They promised *"istiqlal, azadi, hukumat-i islami"* (independence, freedom, Islamic government); yet what you ended up with a swarm of leaches with turbans, repression, and a satanic government. Some of you hoped that a Sunni Taliban in Afghanistan would bring dignity and glory to you. What they brought was worse than the Saudi regime: they put women in black sacks, revived the barbaric stoning practice, regressed to the times of tribalism, denied women education, exponentially increased ignorance, and turned Afghanistan into an international farm for opium. You did not question the religion and sect you inherited from your parents or the teachings of the mullah, the sheikh, or the imam. You little examined the nightmare sold to you as dreams.

We must acknowledge the truth so that the truth will set us free from our own transgression.

God blessed you with crucial natural resources, so that you could utilize it for your prosperity. Yet, their proceeds are wasted by corrupt, hedonistic, shortsighted, backward and oppressive kings, emirs, tribal leaders, and mullahs.

63

Instead of gaining your freedom, instead of establishing the democratic system instructed by the holy book you claim allegiance, you are wasting your time in cafeterias, on the streets, and in rotten offices of antiquity, which produces nothing but zeros.

We must acknowledge the truth so that the truth will set us free from apathy and slavery.

Look at half of your population, your wives, mothers, sisters, daughters. What have you done to them? How can you hope to progress and attain peace, prosperity and God's mercy, while you have buried many of them alive? You cannot expect happiness, while you despise half of God's creation, your wives, mothers, sisters, and daughters; while you deprive them from their human rights given by their Creator, turn them to fractionally humans. You cannot tell God that you did all those evil things to please the idols called Bukhari, Muslim, Tirmizi, Ibn Hanbal, Ibn Maja, Abu Dawud, Malik, Kafi, and a herd of other imams, mullahs and clergymen. None of those idols will save you from God's justice. You are already paying dearly for your misogynistic beliefs and practices. You must apologize to your mothers, wives, sisters, and daughters for treating them like your slaves; you must repent for acting like Pharaohs against them.

We must acknowledge the truth so that the truth will set us free from the dark holes of our deception.

The world knows that Israel has transformed from a victim nation to a racist colonial power. Many progressive Jews too are painfully accepting this fact and they are fighting against it. The world sees and most people acknowledge the fascist policy, occupation, atrocities, massacres, and humiliation committed against the Palestinian people since 1948. The world knows that Israel has killed many more Palestinian children than the Palestinian suicide bombers have done. The numbers and events are out there recorded to prove that Israel has used state terrorism against Palestinian people. The world knows that a coalition of Crusaders, Zionists, and weapon/oil and other interest groups, nested in towers of power are using American tax money, military, and political power to perpetuate this tragedy, hoping for the Armageddon, more land, or bloody profits from wars. Nevertheless, again you must look in the mirror. What have you done, what have you become? You have become as racist as the Zionist you condemn. You condemn Jews without discrimination, Jews that raised many great prophets, philosophers, scientists, and inventors whom you revere and admire. You have become a suicidal nation. Though there were more than mere pacifism into Gandhi's resistance against British colonialism, Gandhi's struggle provided a great example for you. Instead, you followed ignorant leaders, racist and manipulative politicians, terror organizations, misguided religious clerics, and your hormones. If you had taken lessons from modern history and you had used your mind more than your animalistic instincts, if you had followed the Quran rather than the religious teachings that promote violence and racism, by now you would be living next to Israel sharing Jerusalem peacefully as brothers and sisters. You cannot have God's mercy if you respond to hatred with hatred, racism with racism, atrocities with atrocities. You cannot attain freedom and peace without sincerely asking the same thing for your enemies. How can you claim to be muSLiMs, while you have taken SiLM (peace), out of it?

We must acknowledge the truth so that the truth will set us free from violence that has surrounded us.

By continuing along the path of denial and sectarianism, you are risking more than just happiness and dignity in this world, but you also risk shame and retribution in the Hereafter...

> "Those who had rejected will be told: 'God's abhorrence towards you is greater than your abhorrence towards yourselves, for you were invited to acknowledge, but you chose to reject.' They will Say, 'Our Lord, You have made us die twice, and You have given us life twice. Now we have confessed our sins. Is there any way out of this path?' This is because when God Alone was mentioned, you rejected, but when partners were associated with Him, you acknowledged. Therefore, the judgment is for God, the Most High, the Most Great." (40:10-12)

Unless you are willing to take the necessary and painful steps of reform through self-examination and research, you will be led by the mold of complacency and blind followings into the abyss that is becoming your fate. You must turn to the true system of Islam, as revealed by God through His messenger, and stop blindly following your scholars and leaders into distortions and unauthorized teachings. You have been losing continuously because you have abandoned the word of God and replaced it with other religious laws and teachings which in-turn has caused God to abandon you and leave you to your folly.

This life is not just about fun and games...it is about fulfilling our part of the pledge with God and proving that we can serve Him Alone.

> "And when God Alone is mentioned, the hearts of those who do not acknowledge in the Hereafter are filled with aversion; and when others are mentioned beside Him, they rejoice!" (39:45)

Are you ready to embrace the path of God Alone and abandon all your idolatry? Or, will you continue to lose? We must acknowledge the truth so that the truth will set us free.

To the West, Christians, and Americans

The following words are not from an enemy of yours, but from someone who is a member of your society and cares about your interest as much as you care. These are not the words of a politician either, who is ready to break a world record in somersault to appease you; neither the words of a religious leader who lives in a parallel universe of deception and hallucination. These are the words

65

of a common man who left his country behind to seek peace, justice, and liberty. These are the words of a grateful person who found such a refuge in your midst. So, do not treat these words of advice with prejudice, but with care. Do not be scared to hear the truth about your "way of life" which always highlighted the freedom of expression and justice for all. Do not expect me to count the list of the many good things you have accomplished; you hear them frequently from speeches and news in your media, and you celebrate them in your holidays. Sure, you should remember the good things in your past, present, and remember them, so that you can continue repeating those good things. However, you need to hear the other voice too; the voice that you have not yet allocated a holiday to hear. You should open your ears to what you do not hear from those who have invested interest in caressing your ego, nationalism, patriotism, and feelings. I think you do not wish to be aloof to the facts around you and repeat the pattern of all fallen civilizations in history. Do not be arrogant, aloof, self-righteous, and selfish, since they will only inflict you further harm.

We must acknowledge the truth so that the truth will set us free.

Since you have separated the church from state, since you have appreciated the importance of freedom, God has blessed you with progress, abundance and prosperity. Though your history is tainted with wars, oppression, superstitions, and injustices, such as crusades, inquisition, indulgences, sectarian wars, witch-hunt, holocaust, slavery, racism, colonialism, misogynistic practices, sexual abuse, you seem to have learned from the past mistakes and have come up with a better functioning society that tolerates diversity and respects science. Though your society suffers from a myriad of problems such as promiscuous lifestyle, sexually transmitted diseases, high divorce rate, high crimes, videogames teaching violence, addiction with drugs and alcohol, gambling, greed, big gap between rich and poor, children abused by priests, high number of prisoners per capita, homelessness, waste, pollution, jingoism, apathy, etc., your constitutions, courts, congresses, and academic institutions are still functioning. Freedom has its own side effects, and having the freedom of living one's life according to their own choice, without the fear of government repression is by far the greatest value. The greatest danger to your society is the corruption of the democratic process through the influence of money and lobbies. When big corporations control your finance, media, and congress, your democracy and freedom will be only an illusion. However, there is hope, since you frequently demonstrate the confidence to be self-critical and you are able to acknowledge your weaknesses and shortcomings. You have also demonstrated times and again that you have the ability to find novel solutions for social, economic, and political problems. You have shown grace and generosity against your former enemies.

We must acknowledge the truth so that the truth will set us free from self-righteousness.

The world has shrunk due to increase in population, pollution, economic interdependence, mass transportation, and speed and ease in communication;

66

thus, you can no more have a world with half of it eating themselves to obesity while the other half starving to death. You can no more spend billions of dollars on pets, millions of dollars for cosmetic surgeries (including on your pets), gulp world's limited resources to feed your ever-increasing appetite for consuming, and yet expect love and admiration from the rest of the world to your capitalism, the system you adhere to like a religion. How can you convince the world that you are the bastion of liberty while your prison industry is booming and you have the highest number of prisoners per capita in the world? You can no more support cruel, corrupt, regressive puppet regimes and occupying military forces, and expect not being hurt by those who you have deprived directly or indirectly from freedom, education, progress, prosperity and hope. You can no more self-righteously claim to be a free and civilized nation while spending a great portion of your national production on conventional and unconventional weapons, which transforms you into arrogant beasts running from one war to another, from one occupation to another. You can no more fool yourselves to be a peaceful nation while you have been shedding the blood of millions of people around the globe in more than hundred wars, covert operations and occupations in less than a century! You cannot condemn terrorism without apologizing to humanity for destroying not one, but two cities in its entirety as retaliation to an attack of your enemy to your military base. If terrorism means to intimidate the enemy by aiming at civilians, then you should look in the mirror without trying to find justification for your own aggression and acts of terrorism. You cannot talk about a free and better world while you reject banning landmines that kill and maim so many innocent people every day.

We must acknowledge the truth so that the truth will set us free from our own transgression.

Watch out for the right (wrong) wing religious organizations; when they are passionate about a social or political issue think thrice. If their historical record is a measure, they occasionally get it right, but usually they are wrong, very wrong. You cannot let the left-behind fiction fans lead your global policy. However, pay more attention to the other wing, to the other groups, such as Quakers. Their record, their conscience, their heart, their stand for peace and justice, is what you need. We are not telling you to turn your left cheek when you are slapped; but beware of getting intoxicated with power. While you might be pretending to be David, without knowing, your arrogance and transgression might transform you into a Goliath. The change might be slow, so you might not be able to notice it by looking at yourself through the mirror; especially when there are some politician magicians and their entourage whose job is to distort and contort the mirror so that you cannot see yourself as you should.

We must acknowledge the truth so that the truth will set us free from our sins.

You can no more give lip service to the Biblical advice regarding the speck and plank in the eyes. You can no more ignore the fact that those who live by sword are destined to die by the sword. You can no more preach, "Love your enemy" while you are out there trying every means possible to hurt your friends, half-friends, and potential friends. You can no more talk about "the golden rule" while you are working hard to justify the "iron rule" under the euphemistic expression, "preemptory strike." You can no more talk about human rights and freedom while at the same time, you have turned little islands and navy ships into torture centers and you have become the inventors of a diabolic scheme called "offshore interrogation." How come America that once led the establishment of the United Nations and promotion of Human Rights, now has turned torture into an international enterprise and high tech affair? How can you allow the gulags such as, Abu Gharib and Gitmo happen? Yes, you have not broken the records of Stalin, Mao, Hitler, Pol Pot; but you should not be competing with them. Your founding fathers did not fight for independence and did not draft one of the best legal documents in human history so that you become a super war machine and be the cowboy of the world. You carpet bombed dozens of countries in your short history, destroying hundreds of cities and killing millions of them. You destroyed two big cities with its civilian population as retaliation to losing less than three thousands of your soldiers in Pearl Harbor. As retaliation to losing less than three thousand civilians by a terrorist organization, which once you trained and financed, you started two wars, killed hundreds of thousands, destroyed many cities, and are still looking for more countries to destroy. How can you label your revenge, your aggression, your disrespect to the lives of other people, as "freedom" or "civilization"? You cannot change the reality by fabricating fancy names in your PR rooms and spinning them as the corporate media your accomplice. You cannot fool the world by replacing one puppet regime with another, by supporting oppressive and cruel tyrants in Saudi Arabia, Egypt, Pakistan, Israel, and then congratulate yourselves for being the champion of "freedom" and "democracy." You cannot preach about morality, rights, and God, as long as you do not value the lives of each innocent human being equally, regardless of their religion, nationality and color. You have been taking wars, destruction, death, horror and terror to many nations around the world without even changing your fancy lifestyle at home. Now, you are enraged and you demand justice from the world because you have tasted a small fraction of what others have tasted.

We must acknowledge the truth so that the truth will set us free from the dark holes of our deception.

Why should we treat terrorizing an entire nation, destroying their cities, killing, torturing, and humiliating their children and youth in the name of "democracy and liberty" lightly? Why killing tens of thousands of civilians should be forgiven if the murderers, who are also proven congenial liars, use the magic word "collateral damage?" Why smashing the brains of children with bombs or severing their legs and arms should be considered civilized and treated differently than beheadings? Why destroying an entire neighborhood or city and massacring its population by the push of a button from the sky should not be considered equally or more evil than the individual suicide bomber blowing himself or herself up among his powerful enemies who snuffed out all their hope? Why surviving to push another button to kill more people should be considered a civilized action not the action of those who gave their own lives while doing the killing? Why should the smile of a well-fed and well-armed mass murderer be deemed more sympathetic than the pain and anger of a poor person? How can one honestly call an occupying foreign military force to be freedom fighters? How can one call the native population to be terrorists just because they are fighting against an arrogant and lethal occupation army, which was mobilized against them through lies and deception? Why are the children of poor Americans used to kill the children of poor countries?

We must acknowledge the truth so that the truth will set us free from violence that has surrounded us.

You should not favor one criminal over another because of their religion or nationality. Your media did not depict the Serbian rapists and murderers as Christian Murderers, nor they labeled IRA terrorists who engaged in a long sectarian terror campaign that took the lives of thousands, as Christian terrorists. The right wing Christian militia that massacred thousands of Palestinian refugees in Sabra and Shatilla camps somehow lost their religion when they became news on your media. The same with terrorist groups who claimed the cause of Zionism. Furthermore, you should know that state terrorism, regardless of the nationality and religion of the population, is much more cruel, dangerous, and sinister than the group or individual terrorism. In your stand against war, violence, and terrorism, you must be consistent and fair. Peacemakers and promoters must protest and condemn the atrocities regardless as to whether those engaged in atrocities have a uniform on them or not. If military uniform justifies the acts of terror, destruction, or genocide, then Nazi soldiers should receive your sympathy.

We must acknowledge the truth so that the truth will set us free.

One World and Shared Destiny

We must eliminate the nationalistic virus that alienates the children of Adam and turns them into monsters against each other. This does not mean that we should eliminate national borders or abolish the social contracts among groups of people. We must consider the entire world as one community and work accordingly. This is not only morally right, but is the only way we can survive on this little planet. We can no longer be reckless in treating this planet, this precious earth, and can no longer be myopically selfish in our dealings with other nations. Otherwise, we will inhale and poison ourselves with each other's pollution, we will suffer calamities caused by global warming, we will spend a great portion of our national production, we will overpopulate the land, we will shed the blood of many innocent people, and we will lose our individual freedoms for security because of the economic and political problems in other parts of the world. The world has become smaller and troubles are shared more than ever before. We must act now as a world and revive the spirit of the United Nations with a new vision. We can no long afford jingoism, macho attitudes, another world war, always looking for an "evil" outside us, retaliating against violence and terror with our own version of violence and terror. We should not let terrorists or warmongers define our vision, our destiny, since they will only bring more disasters for humanity. We should not allow evil whisperers to dupe us into inflicting another holocaust against another race; we should have learned our lesson. We should not tolerate authoritarian regimes, corrupt leaders, kings, and emirs in our countries; we must be braver than the corrupt bullies. We should be vigilant against the myopic and greedy interest groups that have grown like cancerous tumors in our democracies, infecting legislation, judiciary, executive branches and the mass media.

Hopefully, this century will be the century of unity under the banner of "God Alone," so that the children of Adam will greet each other with peace by saying, "your system/religion is for you and my system/religion is for me." So that, all humanity, including Atheists and polytheists, share this planet in peace and justice.

> "The Lord your God is One God. You shall worship the Lord your God with all your heart, with all your soul, with all your mind, with all your strength." (Old Testament, Deuteronomy 6:4; New Testament, Mark 12:29-30)

> "God bears witness that there is no god but He, as do the angels, and those with knowledge, He is standing with justice. There is no god but Him, the Noble, the Wise." (Quran 3:18)

> "Say, 'O followers of the scripture, let us come to a logical agreement between us and you: that we do not worship except God, that we never set up any idols besides Him, and never set up each other as gods beside God.' If they reject such an agreement, then say, 'Bear witness that we are Submitters.'" (Quran 3:64)

Therefore:

- Let's reject all other religious teachings besides the Quran, and let's dedicate the system to God alone.
- Let's stand against marginal elements among us, oppressive puppet regimes, brutal wars, occupations, and clandestine operations.
- Let's topple the oppressive monarchs, and elect our own leaders so that we can have peace, liberty and justice on our own volition.
- Let's fight not with bullets or bombs, but with intelligence and wisdom.
- Let's give up superstitions and medieval culture, and start engaging in scientific enterprise.
- Let's stop subjugating our mothers, sisters, daughters and wives; let's give them back their dignity, equal rights, liberty, and identity.

- Let's unite our voices and prayers with genuine Christians, Buddhists, Jews, Agnostics, anyone who seeks justice and peace, rather than injustice and war.
- Let's organize local and international conferences to discuss this issue. We may invite religious scholars of every sect or cult, but we should not let them run them, since our experience shows that they have not done a good job in leading.
- Let's acknowledge the truth so that the truth will set us free.

Do These Verses Require us to Follow a Mishmash of Narrations?

(From the *19 Questions for Muslim Scholars* by Edip Yuksel)

Distorting the meaning of the Quranic verses, taking them out of context, claiming that some verses abrogate others are some of the tactics used by the followers of Hadith and Sunna. Monarchist theocratic kingdoms have used the *ulama* to divert "Muslim" masses. The fabricated satanic teachings have transformed the system of God into a mishmash liturgy and a ritual torture. Here, God willing, we will expose their true colors by evaluating some verses most often abused by them.

"Indeed, in the messenger of God a good example has been set for he who seeks God and the Last day and thinks constantly about God." (33:21)

The falsifiers have presented medieval Arab culture and traditions as good examples of the messenger. However, if you look at the context, the good example has been described as the messenger's courage and his constant remembrance of God. They extended this good example to irrelevant individual or cultural behaviors. For instance, they sanctified the beard and turban, ignoring the fact that the Meccan idol worshipers, such as Abu Lahab and Walid b. Mugiyra also had long beards and wore turbans.

What is worse, the actions and words ascribed to prophet Muhammad have depicted him with a character that is far from exemplary. The Hadith books portrays the prophet as a phantasmagoric character with a multiple personality. That character is more fictitious than mythological gods and goddesses, such as Hermes, Pan, Poseidon and Aphrodite. He is a pendulous character, both bouncing up to deity, and down to the lowest degree. He is both wise and moron. He is sometimes more merciful than God and sometimes a cruel torturer. He is both perfect and criminal, humble and arrogant, chaste and sex maniac, trustworthy and cheater, illiterate and educator, rich and poor, a nepotistic and a democratic leader, caring and a male chauvinist, a believer and a disbeliever, prohibiting Hadith and promoting Hadith. You can find numerous conflicting personalities presented as an exemplary figure. Choose whichever you like. This peculiar aspect of Hadith collection is well described by the prophetic verses of the Quran:

> **68:35** Should We treat the ones who peacefully surrendered the same as those who are criminals?
>
> **68:36** What is wrong with you, how do you judge?
>
> **68:37** Or do you have another book which you study?
>
> **68:38** In it, you can find what you wish?

Furthermore, a similar statement is made about Abraham: "A good example has been set for you by Abraham and those with him" (60:4, 6). If verse 33:21 requires Muhammad's hadith, then why would not the verses 60:4,6 require Abraham's hadith? Which books narrate hadiths from Abraham? Obviously, the only reliable source for both examples is the Book of God, which narrates the relevant exemplary actions. It also warns us not to repeat the mistakes committed by Muhammad (33:37; 80: 1-10).

"O you who acknowledge, obey God and obey the messenger and those entrusted amongst you. But if you dispute in any matter, then you shall refer it to God and His messenger, if you acknowledge God and the Last day. That is better and a more suitable solution." (4:59)

Obeying Bukhari, a narrator of lies, is not obeying the messenger. Obeying the messenger is obeying the complete, perfect and fully detailed Quran. Verse 25:73 describes the attitude of believers towards God's revelations.

> **25:73** Those who when they are reminded of their Lord's signs, they do not fall on them deaf and blind.

But the followers of Hadith and Sunna are very good in ignoring them. They do not see 6:19, 7:3, and 50:45 which say that the only teaching delivered by God's messenger was the Quran. They do not think that Muhammad practiced the Quran and the Quran alone (5:48, 49). They do not hear Muhammad's only complaint about his people (25:30). They do not understand that Muhammad disowns those who do not understand that the Quran is enough and fully detailed (6:114).

The first verse of Chapter 9 states that an ultimatum is issued from God an His messenger. We know that the verses about the ultimatum are entirely from God. God did not consult Muhammad about the ultimatum. Muhammad's only mission was to deliver God's message (16:35; 24:54). Thus, the reason that God included the messenger in 9:1 is because he participated as deliverer of the ultimatum, not as the source.

> **9:1** This is an ultimatum from **God** and His messenger to those who set up partners with whom you had entered a treaty.

Similarly, because people receive God's message through messengers we are ordered to obey the messengers. We also know that the Quran is a permanent messenger (65:11), and the Quran is a reminder and deliverer of good news (41:1-4; 11:2).

41:1 H8M40
41:2 A revelation from the Gracious, Compassionate.

41:3 A book whose signs are detailed, a compilation in Arabic for a people who know.

41:4 A bearer of good news, and a warner. But most of them turn away; they do not hear.

"Nor does he speak from personal desire. It is a divine inspiration. (53:3-4)

Meccan idol worshipers claimed that Muhammad was the author of the Quran (25:5; 68:15). The beginning of Chapter 53 is about the revelation of the Quran. It states that "the Quran is from Him". It is not Muhammad's personal claim; it is a divine statement. Therefore, claiming that the pronoun "it" in the verse 53:4 refers to the words of Muhammad, not of God, is an obvious distortion. According to the above verse "it" is revelation, without exception. This can be valid only for the Quran. It is nonsense to claim that Muhammad's daily conversation was entirely revelation. For example, God firmly criticizes Muhammad's words to Zayd (33:37). Obviously, the criticism was not about revelation. The beginning phrase of Chapter 97 informs us about the revelation of the Quran: "We revealed it in the Night of Destiny". The "it" in this verse is the same as the "it" in 53:4.

"With proof and the scriptures... We sent down to you the Reminder to proclaim to the people what was sent to them, and perhaps they would think. (16:44)

People who establish Hadith and Sunna as another source of religious teachings besides the Quran, opted the irrelevant meaning of the Arabic word "BYN". The word *lituBaYyeNa* is a derivative of *BYN*, which is a multiple-meaning word. It means: (1) to reveal what is concealed; (2) to explain what is vague. The first meaning is the antonym of "hide", the second is the antonym of "make vague". God orders Muhammad to proclaim the revelation which is revealed to him personally. Indeed, this is the whole mission of the messengers.

16:35 Those who set up partners said, "If **God** had wished it, we would not have served anything besides Him; neither us nor our fathers; nor would we have forbidden anything without Him." Those before them did the exact same thing; so are the messengers required to do anything but deliver with proof?*

Prophets sometimes experience difficulty in proclaiming the revelation (33:37, 20:25). If the Quran is a profound Arabic book, if it is explained by God, and if it is simple to understand (5:15; 26:195; 11:1; 54:17; 55:1-2), then the prophet does not have an extra mission to explain it. Indeed, the verse 75:19 does not leave any room for an extra human explanation.

75:16 Do not move your tongue with it to make haste.

74

75:17 It is for Us to collect it and relate it.
75:18 So when We relate it, you shall follow its revelation.
75:19 Then it is for Us to clarify it.

Thus, the word *litubayyena* of 16:44 is similar to the one in 3:187.

3:187 God took the covenant of those who were given the book: "You will proclaim to the people and not conceal it." However, they threw it behind their backs and purchased with it a cheap price. Miserable indeed is what they have purchased.

Verse 3:187 tells us that the people who received the revelation should "proclaim the scripture to the people, and never conceal it." Also see 2:159 for another informative contrast.

2:159 Surely those who conceal what We have sent down to them which was clear, and the guidance, after **God** had made it clear in the book; these will be cursed by **God** and be cursed by those who curse;

The Quran is simple to understand (54:11). Whoever opens his/her mind and heart as a monotheist and takes the time to study it, will understand it. This understanding will be enough for salvation. Beyond this, to understand the multi-meaning verses you do not need to be a messenger of God. If you have a good mind and have studied the Quran as a believer, that is, if you have a deep knowledge, then you will be able to understand the true meanings of multiple-meaning verses. The verse 3:7, which is about the multiple-meaning verses, points this fact in a multiple-meaning way: ". . . No one knows their true meaning except God and those who possess knowledge. . ." (This is a very interesting verse with crucial consequences. It is also one of the verses that is mistranslated by almost all translators. I have discussed it extensively in the first chapter of my book: Running Like Zebras.)

"O you who acknowledge, do not advance yourselves before God and His messenger. Be aware of God. God is Hearer, Knowledgeable." (49:1)

Followers of hadith and sunna claim that God is represented by the Quran, and the messenger is represented by his opinion on the Quran. Thus, they claim that the Quran is not enough for salvation. Some people may not utter this claim straightforwardly. They may even claim that the Quran is complete and enough for our guidance. However, further questioning will reveal that their quran is not "the Quran". The Quran is the one that consists of 114 Chapters and 6346 verses. It is a mathematically coded book. However, their minds are confused, and their quran is contaminated with human speculations and limited by a snap-shot interpretation. They try to scare the believers by saying "you do not like the messenger". The belief that God is represented by the Quran, and the messenger by his teaching is a satanic claim. There are several points to remember:

- Quran represents God and His messenger.

- Obeying the Quran is obeying God and the messenger.

- Quran never says: "Obey God and Moses," or "Obey God and Muhammad." But, Quran consistently states: "Obey God and the messenger." This is because the word messenger (rasul) comes from the "message" (risala). The message is entirely from God; messengers cannot exist without the message.

- Messengers as humans make mistakes. Thus, when believers made a covenant with prophet Muhammad they promised to obey him conditionally, i.e., his righteous orders (60:12). Moreover, God specifically orders Muhammad to consult the believers around him (3:159).

> **3:159** It was a mercy from God that you were soft towards them; had you been harsh and mean hearted, they would have dispersed from you; so pardon them and ask forgiveness for them, and consult them in the matter; but when you are convinced, then put your trust in God; God loves those who trust.

- If nobody can object to the personal decision of the messenger, then consultation is meaningless. However, whenever the final decision is made, it should be followed.

- During their lifetimes, messengers are community leaders. In this regard messengers are not different than the believers who are in charge (4:59); both should be obeyed. But, this obedience is not absolute. It is open for consultation and discussion.

- The position of messengers are different during their lives; they are interactive teachers and curious students as well. We have the chance to ask them further questions, discuss issues, learn their intention, and even correct their mistakes. On the other hand, they have the opportunity to correct our misunderstandings. However, when they pass away their teaching becomes frozen and looses its advancing three-dimensional character. The frozen, snap-shot fragments of knowledge are a dangerous weapon in the hand of ignorant people to stop God's teachings. They defend every plain error in the name of the messenger. They insult every sincere students of God's revelation.

"... Say, 'I do not ask you for any wage, except that you show compassion to your relatives.'..." (42:23)

This verse is mostly abused by Shiite Muslims. They claim that prophet Muhammad was ordered to ask help for HIS relatives. This distortion created a class of blood sucking people surviving on charity. Hundreds of thousands of people in Iran, Iraq and other Middle Eastern countries claim that they are descendants of Prophet Muhammad (*Sayyeed* or *Shareef*) and they are entitled to obligatory financial help. They abuse the verse mentioned above to exploit people economically. However, the verse does not say "my relatives". The context of the verse is plain enough to state that Muhammad does not need a wage from the believers and if they can help somebody they should help their own relatives. Indeed, helping the relatives is a divine command repeated in 2:83; 4:36; 8:41; 16:90.

> 4:36   Serve God and do not set up anything with Him, and be kind to the parents, and the relatives, and the needy, and the neighbor who is of kin, and the neighbor next door, and close friend, and the traveler, and those with whom you have contractual rights. God does not like the arrogant, the boastful.

The special status given to the descendants of Muhammad through Fatima and Ali has created a privileged and "sacred" religious class who exploits their followers politically, economically and mentally. For mere political reasons, the Shiite scholars with do not consider Muhammad's wife Aisha as a member of his family! Bizarre!

Eager to Fabricate Alternative Revelations

Muslim clerics claim that a part of revelation to Prophet Muhammad was preserved word for word under the title of the Quran. All other "revelation," according to them, was embodied either in the Prophet's sayings or in his practices which were "carefully preserved" by the Companions as the Sunna of the Prophet Muhammad. The following verses are abused for the purposes of raising the volumes of hadith fabrications to the level of the Quran:

"As such, We have made you a balanced/impartial nation so that you may be witnesses over the people, and that the messenger may be witness over you. We did not make the focal point that you came on except so that we know who follows the messenger from those who will turn on their heels. It was a big deal indeed except for those whom God had guided; God was not

to waste your acknowledgement. God is Kind and Compassionate over the people." (2:143)

Sunni clergymen claim that God Himself had appointed Jerusalem as the initial Qiblah (i.e. direction faced when praying) for the Prophet in the past and there is no verse in the Quran which commands the Prophet to face Jerusalem at the beginning of his mission. Therefore, they continue, the Prophet must have received this guidance from God in a form other than the Quran. They claim that this alternative revelation has been preserved in the Sunna.

A careful study of the verses in their context reveals the distortion of Sunni scholars. Muhammad was ordered by the Quranic verses to switch his qibla to Mecca (not to Jerusalem), and this revelation ordering believers to turn back to Mecca was the test, not the other way around.

The "change" referred in 2:142 is not about changing to Jerusalem but it is about changing to Mecca. After escaping from Meccan oppressors, prophet Muhammad and believers decided to change the *qibla* to Jerusalem, as a sign of good relation with Christian community in Medina. Since there was no expressed divine commandment at that time, they considered it as a discretionary matter. However, when God Almighty ordered them to turn back to Kaba in Mecca, it became a distinguishing test for the Muslim community. Some could not accept this divine commandment, since they have established strong social and economic ties with Christians and Jews in Medina. They wanted to please them (2:145). Thus, God Almighty uses this issue to expose hypocrites.

In brief, there was no revelation out of the Quran requiring believers to follow. The revelation that was testing the Muslim community was the very verses 2:142-146. Verse 2:145 clearly explains the nature of the test. Those who preferred pleasing Christians, instead of following the revelation, had difficulty in turning back to Mecca.

"When the Prophet disclosed a matter in confidence to one of his wives, and she then spread it, God made it known to him. He confirmed a part of it and repudiated a part. Then when he informed her, she said, 'Who informed you of this?' He said, 'I was informed by the Omniscient, Most Cognizant.'"66:3

Sunni scholars asks, "How did God make it known to him and tell him?" They claim that he learned about this issue not via the Quran, since there is no mention of it anywhere else in the Book of God. Therefore, they conclude, the Prophet must have been told via revelation from God which is not part of the Quran.

78

"It is we who will collect it into Quran. Once we recite it, you shall follow such a Quran." (75:17-18)

Eager to find "alternative revelations" to the Quran, *mushrik* scholars develop arguments on unpredictable verses. This is one of them. They acknowledge that God took it upon Himself to collect the Quran. They argue that Prophet directed the scribes of the Quran to arrange its suras (chapters) in the order found today; this is not the order in which they were revealed. Therefore, since this was God's responsibility, it shows that He guided the Prophet with respect to the order of the *sura*.

AN ANALOGY

The Quran broadcasts a very clear message. However, the problem is with our receivers. If our receiver does not hear the broadcast or cannot understand it well, then something is wrong with our receiver and we have to check it. If the signal is weak, we need to recharge our batteries, or reset our antennas. If we do not receive a clear message, we need to tune into the station, to the station of Quran alone, in order to get rid of the noises and interference from other sources. We may ask some help from knowledgeable people or experts for this task. If the receiver does not work at all, then we have to make a sincere effort to fix the broken parts. However, if we believe that the problem is in the broadcast, then nobody can help us. The divine broadcast can be heard in detail only by those who sincerely tune in, i.e., those who take it seriously and act accordingly.

The condition of our receiver and the antenna, the power of the battery, and the precision level of our tuning are very important in getting the divine message properly.

DETAILED QUESTIONS

2.1. If the verse 33:21 requires Muhammad's hadith, then why would not the verses 60:4,6 require Abraham's hadith? Which books narrate hadiths from Abraham?

2.2. You try to justify your collections of hadiths by using 33:21. Ironically, your collections do not provide an exemplary character. How can you claim that an eye-gouger, a urine-prescriber, a sex maniac is a "good example"?

2.3. The Quran states "Obey God and the messenger." How can you twist this commandment and make Bukhary, or Al-Kafy and many other story books as the second source of Islam? According to verse 4:59 we have to obey the people in charge too. Thus, does it mean that Islam is a co-authored religion by at least three sources?

2.4. The first verse of Chapter 9 states that an ultimatum is issued from God an His messenger. We know that the verses about the ultimatum are entirely from God. Muhammad was not the co-author of the ultimatum. Muhammad's only mission was to deliver God's message (16:35; 24:54). Thus, the reason that God includes the messenger in verse 9:1 is the messenger's participation as a deliverer of the ultimatum. Why don't you apply this explanation to other verses where the word "messenger" is mentioned after God?

2.5. Why do you distort the meaning of 53:3,4 by taking it out of context?

2.6. By claiming that it is the mission of the messenger to explain the Quran, you contradict 16:35; 55:2; 75:19 and many other verses. In order to support your claim you opt a different meaning of *litubayyena* in 16:44. In fact, the word *litubayyena* of 16:44 is no different than the ones in 3:187 and 2:159. This verse tells us that the people who received the revelation should "proclaim the scripture to people, and never conceal it." How can you claim that the meaning of *litubayyena* in 16:44 is "to explain", but not "to proclaim"?

2.7. You have created a privileged class out of descendents of the prophet Muhammad by misinterpreting 42:23. What are the Arabic equivalence of "the relatives" and "my relatives"? Which one is mentioned in that verse?

"How Can we Observe the *Sala* Prayers by Following the Quran Alone?"

"How can we observe the *Sala* prayers by following the Quran alone?" is a favorite question among the adherents of Sunni and Shiite sects who follow derivative texts, religious instruction, teachings and laws, all of which were authored by men. With this question, both sects try to justify the necessity and proliferation of contradictory sectarian teachings, medieval Arab culture, oppressive laws filled with numerous prohibitions and regulations--all falsely attributed to God and His prophet. Perhaps, the best answer for those who direct that question is the following:

If you are expecting the intercession of Muhammad and many other saints, if you are associating your religious leaders as partners to God in authoring your system, justifying authoritarian regimes, violating women's rights and putting them in black sacks, showing no tolerance for the expression of opposing ideas and cultures, justifying the punishment of stoning to death for adulterers, adhering to numerous superstitions, entering the restroom with left foot, forcing your child to eat with right hand, prohibiting music and visual arts..... In short, if you are condemning yourself and your society to a backward and miserable life just because you learn from those sectarian sources how to bend your belly or where to put your hands, then it is better for you not to pray at all. Such a prayer (more accurately, physical exercise), is not worth exchanging monotheism with polytheism, reason with ignorance, light with darkness, peace with conflicts, universalism with tribalism, progress with regression.

But, this answer may not be able to wake them up and save them from the cobwebs of clergymen. They will still challenge us to produce a manual for prayer. How and how many times to bow, where and how to put their hands, what to do with their fingers, where and how to stand on their feet, etc. For many adherents of Sunni or Shiite sects, the question is just an excuse to avoid the pain of reforming themselves. They know that the Quran does not provide extensive explanation on every itsy bitsy spiders crawling in their minds. So, the question is usually asked in a rhetorical sense: "You cannot find in the Quran how many times to bow and prostrate, or how to hold my index or pinki finger in *Sala* prayer, so I will continue following all those volumes of contradictory books filled with silly stories and outrageous instructions!"

As a result, Monotheism is redefined as a Limited Partnership, in which the recognition and submission to God alone becomes an oxymoron; a contradiction in terms in which other 'partners' are submitted to and accepted by these 'believers.' The most common set-up for Sunni *shirk* is: the Quran (God) +

*hadith*s and *sunna* (messenger) + the practice of the Prophet's companions + the practice of the companions of the Prophet's companions + the opinions of emams (ijtihad) + consensus of *ulama* in a particular sect (*ijma'*) + the comments and opinions of their students + the comments and opinions of early *ulama* + the comments and opinions of later *ulama* + the fatwas of living *ulama*.

In Shiite version of *shirk*, in addition to the aforementioned partners, the 12 Infallible Emams (all relatives and descendants of the Prophet Muhammad starting with Ali) and the living substitute emam is added to the board of directors of the Holy Limited Partnership. The Quran is usually considered an ambiguous book and is basically distorted and aused for their justification of this *shirk*, that is, setting partners with God.

Islam, which means Submission to God in peace, is the state of mind of all people who submit to God alone. All messengers, Noah, Abraham, Moses, Solomon, Jesus and all previous monotheists were Submitters (2:131; 5:111; 7:126; 10:72,84; 22:78; 27:31,42,91; 28:53; 72:14). Thus, the only system approved by God is Submission to God (3:19). It is God Almighty who uses this attribute to describe those who submit to His law (22:78). Islam is referred to as the "System of Abraham" in many verses since Meccan idol worshipers were claiming that they were following their father Abraham (2:130,135; 3:95; 4:125; 6:161; 12:37-38; 16:123; 21:73; 22:78). And Muhammad was a follower of Abraham (16:123).

Ignorant of the fact that Abraham observed the contact prayers (21:73), many contemporary muslims challenge God by asking where we can find the number of units in each contact prayer. Ignorant of the fact that God claimed Quran to be complete (6:11-116), they do not "see" that ALL religious practices of Submission/Monotheism were established and practiced before the Quranic revelation (8:35; 9:54; 16:123; 21:73; 22:27; 28:27). Messengers after Abraham practiced *Sala* prayers, obligatory charity, and fasting (2:43; 3:43; 11:87; 19:31,59; 20:14; 28:27; 31:17).

The Meccan mushriks used to believe that they were followers of Abraham. They were not worshipping statutes or icons as claimed by *hadith* fabricators, but they were praying for *shafaat* (intercession) from some holy names, such as al-Lat, al-Uzza, and al-Manaat (53:19-23). So, contrary to their false assertion of being monotheists (6:23), they were accused of being *mushrik* or associating partners to God (39:3).

Sunni and Shiite scholars subsequently fabricated stories in an attempt to erase any similarities between themselves and the mushriks, but in doing so exposed their own inherent lies in contradictory descriptions of those statutes (For instance, see Al-Kalbi's classic book on statutes: Kitab-ul Asnam). Meccan mushriks who were proud of Abraham's legend could not practice the literal observance of idol-worship; they settled for a more metaphysical satanic trap by

82

accepting intercession and man-made religious prohibitions (6:145-150; 39:3). They were metaphysical or spiritual idol worshipers.

Meccan *Mushriks*, during the era of Prophet Muhammad were respecting the Sacred *Masjid* built by Abraham (9:19). They were practicing the contact prayers, fasting, and pilgrimage (2:183,99; 8:35–the meaning of this verse is deliberately distorted in traditional translations–; 9:54; 107:4-6). Although they knew *Zaka* (obligatory charity) they were not fulfilling their obligation (53:34). During the time of the Prophet Muhammad people knew the meaning of *Sala, Zaka, Sawm,* and *Hajj.* They were not foreign words.

God sent the Quran in their language. As with each proceeding Book, the revelation was given in it's time, in the language of the people receiving the revelation. God commands and reveals in a manner which can be both understood and observed, and then He details His requirements of His people throughout His Book (16:103; 26:195). Moreover, if God wants to add a new meaning to a known word, He informs us. For instance, the Arabic word *al-din* in 1:4 is explained in 82:15-19.

Verse 16:123 is a direct proof that all religious practices in Islam were intact when Muhammad was born. Thus, he was ordered to "follow the system of Abraham." If I ask you to ride a bicycle, it is assumed that you know what a bicycle is and you know or would learn from others how to ride it. Similarly, when God enjoined Muhammad to follow the practices of Abraham (16:123), such practices must have been well known.

Nevertheless, contrary to the popular belief, the Quran details contact prayers. While neither Quran nor *hadith* books contain illustration for *Sala* or video clips showing how the prophets observed their *Sala,* Quran does describe prayer. The Quranic description of *Sala* prayer is much more superior for the following reasons:

- The language of the Quran is superior to the language of *hadith*s. *Hadith*s are collections of narration containing numerous different dialects and are inflicted with chronic and endemic linguistic problems. The language of the Quran is much simpler as witnessed by those who study both the Quran and *hadith*. The eloquence of the Quranic language is emphasized in the Quran with a repeated rhetorical question (54:17, 22, 32, 40).

- *Hadith* books may contain more details. But are those details helpful and consistent with the Quran? How does a believer decide between conflicting details? Does he just pick the word of his favorite Imam? If we follow the words of a particular, favorite imam, does that mean that we are really following the practice of the prophet? For instance, you may find dozens of *hadith*s in Sahih Muslim narrating that the Prophet Muhammad read the first chapter of the Quran, al-Fatiha, and bowed down, without reading any additional verses from the Quran. You will

83

find many other *hadith*s claiming that the Prophet read this or that chapter after al-Fatiha. There are also many conflicting *hadith*s regarding ablution which is the source of different rituals among sects. *Hadith*, more or less of them compounding God's Word with contradictory details, cannot guide to the truth. It has become a necessary evil for ignorant believers and community leaders who manipulate them.

- *Hadith* books narrate a silly story regarding the times of *Sala* prayer and its ordinance. The story of Mirage is one of the longest *hadith*s in the Bukhari. Reportedly, after getting frequent advice from Moses by going up and down between the sixth and seventh heaven, Muhammad negotiated with God to reduce the number of prayers from 50 times a day (one prayer for every 28 minutes) to 5 times a day. This *hadith* portrays Muhammad as a compassionate union leader saving his people from God's unmerciful and impossible demand.

SALA PRAYER ACCORDING TO THE QURAN

- Observing *Sala* prayer is frequently mentioned together with giving charity and thus emphasizing the social consciousness and communal responsibility of those who observe the prayer (2:43,83,110; 4:77; 22:78; 107:1-7).
- *Sala* prayer is observed to commemorate and remember God alone (6:162; 20:14).
- *Sala* remembrance protects us from sins and harming others (29:45).
- *Sala* prayer should be observed continuously until death (19:31; 70:23,34).
- *Sala* is for God's remembrance (20:14).
- *Sala* is conducted regularly at three times each day (24:58, 11:114, 2:238, 17:78).
- *Sala* is for men and women (9:71).
- *Sala* requires a sober state of mind (4:43).
- *Sala* requires cleanliness (5:6).
- *Sala* is done while facing one unifying point (2:144).
- *Sala* is done in a stationary standing position (2:238-239).
- *Sala* involves the oath being made to God (1:1-7) followed by the Scripture being recited (29:45).
- *Sala* requires a moderate voice (17:110).
- *Sala* involves prostration (4:102).
- *Sala* is ended by prostrating and saying specific words (4:102, 17:111).
- *Sala* can be shortened in case of war (4:101).
- *Sala* can be done on the move or sitting in case of worry (2:239).
- *Sala* is to be prescribed to your own family (20:133).
- *Sala* is also performed with congregation (62: 9-10).

Ablution

To observe prayer one must make ablution (4:43; 5:6). Ablution is nullified only by sexual intercourse or passing urine or defecation. Ablution remains valid even if one has passed gas, shaking hands with the opposite sex, or a woman is menstruating. A menstruating woman may observe contact prayers, contrary to superstitious cultural beliefs (5:6; 2:222; 6:114-115).

Dress Code

There is not a particular dress code for prayer, in fact, if you wish you may pray nude in your privacy. Covering our bodies is a social and cultural necessity aimed to protect ourselves from harassment, misunderstanding and undesired consequences (7:26; 24:31; 33:59).

Times for Prayer

Quran mentions three periods of time in conjunction with *Sala* prayer. In other words, the Quran qualifies the word "*Sala*" by three different temporal words: (1) *Sala*-al Fajr (Morning Prayer), (2) *Sala*-al Esha (Evening Prayer), (3) *Sala*-al Wusta (Middle Prayer). The Morning Prayer (24:58) and Night Prayer (24:58) should be observed at both ends of the day and part of the night (11:114). (We will discuss the times of *Sala* prayers later in detail at the end of this article).

Direction for Prayer

For the prayer one should face the Sacred Masjid built by Abraham, the Ka'ba (2:125, 143-150; 22:26). To find the correct qibla a person should keep in mind that the world is a globe, far different from Mercator's flat map. Since the prayer during emergency and fear is reduced to one unit, in normal conditions the prayer should be at least two units and during the prayer one must dramatically reduce his/her contact with the external world (4:101-103). Prayers, unlike fasting, cannot be performed later after they are missed; they must be observed on time (4:103).

Congregational Prayer

Believers, men and women, once a week are invited to a particular location to pray together every *Juma* (Congregational) Day. They go back to their work and normal daily schedule after the Congregational Prayer which could be led by either man or a woman (62:9-11). The mosques or masjids should be dedicated to God alone, thus, the invitation should be restricted to worship God alone, and no other name should be inscribed on the walls of masjids and none other than God should be commemorated (72:18-20). Those who go to masjids should dress nicely since masjids are for public worship and meetings (7:31).

Position for Prayer

One should start the *Sala* prayer in standing position (2:238; 3:39; 4:102) and should not change his/her place except during unusual circumstances, such as

85

while riding or driving (2:239). Submission to God should be declared physically and symbolically by first bowing down and prostrating (4:102; 22:26; 38:24; 48:29). This physical ritual is not required at the times of emergencies, fear, and unusual circumstances (2:239).

Comprehension and Purpose of Prayer

We must comprehend the meaning of our prayers, as these are the moments in which we communicate directly with God (4:43). We must be reverent during our contact prayers (23:2). Along with understanding what we say, we can recall one of God's attributes, depending on our need and condition during the time of our prayer (17:111). Prayer is to commemorate God, and God Alone (6:162; 20:14; 29:45). Prayer is to praise, exalt and remember His greatness, His Mercy and ultimately our dependence on each of these attributes (1:1-7; 20:14; 17:111; 2:45). So that even mentioning other names besides God's contradicts our love and dependence on Him (72:18; 29:45).

Recitation during the *Sala* Prayer

Preferring the Quran for recitation has practical benefits since believers from all around the world can pray together without arguing on which language to chose or which translation to use. The chapter al-Fatiha (The Opening) is the only chapter which addresses God in its entirety and is an appropriate prayer for *Sala*. For non-Arabs it should not be too difficult to learn the meaning of words in al-Fatiha, since it consists of seven short verses. Those who are unable to learn the meaning of al-Fatiha should pray in the language that he or she understands. I see no practical reason for reciting in Arabic during individually observed prayers.

We should recite *Sala* prayers in moderate tone, and we should neither try to hide our prayers nor try to pray it in public for political or religious demonstration (17:111). If it is observed with congregation, we should listen to the recitation of the men or women who leads the prayer (7:204; 17:111). After completing the *Sala* prayer, we should continue remembering God (4:103).

Units of Prayer

The Quran does not specify any number of units for prayers. It leaves it to our discretion. We may deduce some ideas regarding the length of the prayers from verses 4:101 and 102. Verse 101 allows us to shorten our prayers because of the fear of being ambushed by enemy during wars. The following verse explains how to pray with turn; it mentions only one prostration, thus implying one unit. If shortening the prayers is considered as reducing the number of their units, then one may infer that prayers at normal times should consist at least of two units. The units of the Congregational Prayer being 2 are revealing, since it is more likely to be accurately preserved. Again, the units of prayer are not fixed by the Quran; it is up to individual and groups.

86

Funeral Prayer

There is no funeral *Sala* prayer. However, remembering those who died as monotheists and providing community support for their relatives is a civic duty.

Sectarian Innovations

There are many sectarian innovations that differ from sect to sect. Some of the innovations are: combining the times of prayers, performing the prayers omitted at their proper times, shortening the prayers during normal trips, adding extra prayers such as *sunna* and *nawafil*, innovating a paid cleric occupation to lead the prayers, prohibiting women from leading the prayers, while sitting reciting a prayer "*at-Tahiyat*" which addresses to the Prophet Muhammad as he is alive and omnipresent, adding Muhammad's name to the *Shahada*, reciting *zamm-us Sura* (extra chapters) after the *al-Fatiha*, indulging in sectarian arguments on details of how to hold your hands and fingers, washing mouth and nose as elements of taking ablution, brushing the teeth with *misvak* (a dry branch of a three beaten into fibers at one end as a toothbrush) just before starting the prayers, wearing turbans or scarves to receive more credits...

HOW MANY PRAYERS A DAY?

Only three Contact Prayers are mentioned by name in the Quran. In other words, the word "*Sala*" is qualified with descriptive words in three instances. These are:

    1. *Sala-al Fajr*-DAWN PRAYER   (24:58; 11:114).
    2. *Sala-al Esha*-EVENING PRAYER (24:58; 17:78; 11:114)
    3. *Sala-al Wusta*- MIDDLE PRAYER (2:238; 17:78)

All of the verses that define the times of the prayers are attributable to one of these three prayers. Now let's see the related verses:

DAWN & EVENING PRAYERS by their names:

"... This is to be done in three instances: before the DAWN PRAYER, at noon when you change your clothes to rest, and after the EVENING PRAYER..." (24:58).

For other usage of the word "esha" (evening) see: 12:16; 79:46

The times of DAWN & EVENING PRAYERS defined:

"You shall observe the contact prayers at both ends of the daylight, that is, during the adjacent hours of the night..." (11:114)

Traditional translators and commentators consider the last clause "*zulfan minal layl*" of this verse as a separate prayer indicating to the "night" prayer. However, we consider that clause not as an addition but as an explanation of the previous ambiguous clause; it explains the temporal direction of the ends of the day. The limits of "Nahar" (daylight) is marked by two distinct points: sunrise and sunset.

In other words, two prayers should be observed not just after sunrise and before sunset, but before sunrise and after sunset.

Furthermore, the traditional understanding runs into the problem of contradicting the practice of the very tradition it intend to promote. Traditionally, both morning and evening prayers are observed in a time period that Quranically is considered *LaYL* (night) since *Layl* starts from sunset and ends at sunrise. The word *Layl* in Arabic is more comprehensive than the word "night" used in English.

If the expression *tarafayin nahar* (both ends of the day) refers to morning and evening prayers which are part of *Layl* (night), then, the last clause cannot be describing another prayer time.

The time of NOON and EVENING PRAYER defined.

> "You shall observe the contact prayer when the sun goes down until the darkness of the night. You shall also observe the Quran at dawn. Reading the Quran at dawn is witnessed." (17:78).

The decline of the sun can be understood either its decline from the zenith marking the start of the Noon prayer or its decline behind the horizon marking the start of the Evening prayer. There are two opposing theories regarding the purpose of the usage of "duluk" (rub) in the verse; nevertheless, either understanding will not contradict the idea of 3 times a day since both Noon and Evening prayers are accepted.

MIDDLE PRAYER (Noon)

> "You shall consistently observe the contact prayers, especially the MIDDLE PRAYER, and devote yourselves totally to God." (2:238).

Verse 38:32 implies that the time of the Middle prayer ends with sunset.

We can easily understand the MIDDLE prayer as a prayer between the two other prayers mentioned by name (Dawn and Evening).

The Old Testament has at least three verses referring to Contact Prayers (*Sala*) and they confirm this understanding. Though we may not trust the Biblical translations verbatim, we may not consider them as errors since both internal and external consistency of the Biblical passages regarding the Contact Prayers are striking.

> "And as soon as the lad was gone, David arose out of a place toward the south, and fell on his face to the ground, and bowed himself three times: and they kissed one another, and wept one with another, until David exceeded." (1 Samuel 20:41)

> "As for me, I will call upon God; and the Lord shall save me. Evening, and morning, and at noon, will I pray, and cry aloud: and he shall hear my

88

voice." (Psalms 55:16-17) (PS: crying aloud apparently means praying with passion).

"Now when Daniel knew that the writing was signed, he went into his house; and his windows being open in his chamber toward Jerusalem, he kneeled upon his knees three times a day, and prayed, and gave thanks before his God, as he did aforetime." (Daniel 6:10)

The followers of Shiite sect observe 5 prayers in 3 times: morning, noon and evening. This strange practice perhaps was the result of a historical compromise with the dominant Sunni 5-times-a-day practice.

***

ADDENDUM (2009)

Though the 3 times of prayer is my current understanding, I do not find fault in praying five times a day. Since we have decided to devote ourselves to God alone and uphold the Quran alone as a sufficient authority for eternal guidance, we have exposed and rejected numerous false teachings. During this process of purification, we have been passing through internal debate, both individually and as groups. The debate on Sala, prayer have been one of the longest lasting and more contentious. Sometimes, we tend to ignore our agreement on so many issues and focus on our differences. I have received accusations of being a "divider" from some of the followers of the Quran alone as divine source, and engaged in numerous debates on this issue.

With bigotry and expectation that everyone must understand everything exactly like we do has been one of the main causes of division. Furthermore, the great majority of those who follow the Quran alone as divine source have so much in common... But the dividers focus on the marginal ones and focus on the few issues that are still being discussed: they scream division! Their obsession with the military-style lock-step and uniform walk is perhaps the very cause of the division they complain about...

If we make different understandings/practices of a detail that is not even mentioned in the Quran (such as *rakaas*, that is units of the *sala* prayers, or the position of our hands during standing in *sala*), as the cause of hostility and division among ourselves then we are doomed to be divided into many sects and sub-sects. Interestingly, we are following a book that contains verse 2:62 among others.

May God guide us, teach us, and help us to show the courage and wisdom to accept the truth and correct ourselves. 20.114.

Why Trash All the *Hadiths* as Secondary Authority Besides the Quran?

After witnessing the comparison between the *hadith* and the Quran, how can a sound mind still insist on *hadith*? How can people still call those books *sharif* (honorable), or *sahih* (authentic)? How can they forgive the *hadith* narrators and collectors who sold them all kinds of lies and stories, containing so much ignorance and distortion? How can they get mad at Salman Rushdi, while much worse insults charged against Muhammad by *hadith* narrators and collectors?

When followers of *hadith* and *sunna* cannot defend the nonsensical and contradictory *hadiths* (narrations) abundant in their so-called authentic *hadith* books, they suggest picking and choosing those *hadiths* that are not contradictory to the Quran. The following brief argument with a Sunnite shows how deceptive and meaningless this apparently innocent suggestion. We call these people compromisers, or Selective Sunnis. Let's now follow a debate between a Selective Sunni and a Monotheist Muslim:

Sunni:

1. How can you claim that several thousand *sahih hadiths* are necessarily false while you cite only a few *sahih hadiths* which have debatable contents? Is this not generalization from scanty data?

2. Why do you assume that either all *sahih hadiths* should be rejected or all of them should be accepted? Why not judge each *hadith* based on its individual merit according to all the available data about its *isnad*, its transmitters, and so on?

3. Suppose we cease to use *hadith* as a source of information about the Prophet, his life, and his career. Then we notice that the Quran itself says very little about the Prophet's life. It also says nothing about how it was complied.

4. The historicity of the Quran is based on *hadiths*. It is from *hadiths* that we know how the Quran was complied. It is also from *hadith* that we know about the life of the Prophet.

Muslim:

1. If any book contains a few lies (and we have more than just "a few"), then, the endorsement of that book is not reliable. If you see dozens of repeated fabrications introduced as trustworthy (*sahih*) *hadith*, then how can you still rely on other narrations of the same book? How can you trust Bukhari, Muslim, and Ibn Hanbal who narrate the LAST *HADITH* of the prophet Muhammad in his death bed, rejecting the recording of any *hadith* through a declaration from the mouth of Omar Bin Khattab and the acquiescence of all prominent muslims that

90

"*Hasbuna kitabullah*" (God's book is enough for us)? (Bukhari: Itisam 26, Ilm 39,49, Janaiz 32, Jihad 176, Jizya 6, Marza 17, Magazi 83; Muslim, Janaiz 23, Vassiya 20-22; Hanbal 1/222,324,336,355).

2. Judging each *hadith* on its individual merit may seem attractive for those who are not satisfied with God's book, but it is a waste of time and a deceptive method. If the signature of narrators (*sanad*) cannot provide authenticity about the source of *hadith*, then our only guide to decide on the content of *hadith*s (*matn*) will be our personal wish or our current inclinations. How can we decide which *hadith* has merit? How can we decide which *hadith* is accurate? We may say "by comparing them with the Quran!" But, what does this really mean? If it is "me" who will compare a *hadith* to the Quran, if it is again "me" who will ultimately judge whether it contradicts the Quran or not, then, I will end up with "*hadith*" which supports "my" personal understanding of the Quran. In this case a *hadith* cannot function as an explanation of the Quran. It will be confirmation or justification of my or someone else's understanding of the Quran; with literally tasteless, grammatically lame language.... Furthermore, what about *hadith*s that bring extra duties and prohibitions?

3. Again, there are many *hadith*s about the prophet's life, which you cannot accept with a sober mind. They are narrated repeatedly in many so-called authentic books. We cannot create a history out of a mishmash of narration by a subjective method of pick and choose. We can create many conflicting portraits of Muhammad out of those *hadith*s. As for pure historical events that are isolated from their moral and religious implications, they are not part of the system, and we don't need them for our salvation. I never said "we should not read *hadith*." In fact, we may study *hadith* books to get an approximate idea about the people, culture and events of those times. We can even construct a "conjecture" about the history, without attributing them to God or his prophet. Please don't forget that "history" is not immune to filtration, censorship and distortion by the ruling class. You can see many different versions of histories (!) regarding the era of early Islam. Just read Sunni and Shiite histories.

4. We cannot disregard God's frequent assertion that the Quran is sufficiently detailed, complete, clear, and easy to understand. What do you think about the verse 12:111? "In their stories is a lesson for the people of intelligence. It is not a *hadith* that was invented, but an authentication of what is already present, a detailing of all things, and a guidance and mercy to a people who acknowledge." Or, what about 17:46? "When you preach your Lord, in the Quran ALONE, they run away with aversion."

5. *Hadith* books are full of contradictory teachings. They eventually lead us to a sanctified and justified sectarian division in the name of the Prophet. Their very nature is another proof that *hadith* collections cannot be divine, since God, characterizes his word and system as not having contradiction: "Why do they not study the Quran careful? If it were from other than God, they would have found in it numerous contradictions." (4:82). This verse clearly refutes the traditional

91

argument that *hadith* books contain other revelations besides the Quran, since the followers of *Hadith* and *Sunna* confuse some of the reference to Quran with *hadith*, as in: "Your friend (Muhammad) is not astray, nor is he deceived. Nor is he speaking out of a personal desire. It is a divine inspiration." (53:2-4). Furthermore, verses 39:27-28 describe the Quran and the following verse distinguishes the divine teaching from other teachings. "God cites the example of a man who deals with disputing partners, compared to a man who deals with only one man. Are they the same? Praise be to God; most of them do not know." (39:29). Obviously, *hadith* narrators and collections are "disputing partners," while the Quran is a consistent source.

6. Our conviction regarding the divinity of the Quran and even its protection does not come from our trust in the number of people, but from the evidence contained in the book, which is another number, a number that is not appreciated by those who determine the truth based on the number of heads with turbans. (Wonder about that number? See 74:30).

7. We reject *Hadith* because we respect Muhammad. No sound person would like to have people born several centuries after him roam the earth and collect a bunch of hearsay attributed to him. Besides, if Muhammad and his supporters really believed that the Quran was not sufficient for guidance, an ambiguous book, or lacked details, then, surely they would be the first ones who would write them down and collect them in books. After all, their numbers were in tens of thousands and they had plenty of wealth. They could afford some ink, papyrus paper or leather, and some brain cells, for such an important task. They would not leave it for a guy from far Bukhara or his ilk who would come more than two hundred years to collect *hadith*s in a land soaked with blood because of sectarian wars. Besides, Muhammad had many unemployed or handicapped people around who could gladly volunteer for such mission. The traditional excuse fabricated for Prophet Muhammad and his supporters is absurd. Supposedly, Muhammad and his followers feared that people would mix the Quran with *hadith*s. This is nonsense. They were smart enough to distinguish both, and there were enough people to keep track of them. Besides, what is the use of separating both, if we will need the second for our salvation as much as we need the first? In practice, the followers of *Hadith* have perfectly mixed both. Worse, in most instances they have preferred *hadith* over the Quran.

Furthermore, it is the followers of *hadith* and *sunna* themselves who claim that the Quran was a "literary miracle". If their claim of "literary miracle" were true, then it would be much easier to separate the verses of the Quran from *hadith*. Let's assume that they could not really distinguish the text of the Quran from Muhammad's words, then couldn't they simply mark the pages of the scripture with the letter Q for the Quran and letter H for *Hadith*, or let some record only the Quran, or simply color code their covers? Or allocate leather for the Quran and paper for *hadith*, or vise versa? They could find many ways to keep different books separate from each other. They did not need to study rocket science or have computer technology to accomplish that primitive task. The collectors of *hadith*s wished that people would accept their assertion that Muhammad and his supporters did not have ink, paper or leather, mind, and care to collect *hadith* before them. No wonder, they even fabricated a few *hadith*s claiming that Muhammad's companions were competing with dogs for bones to write on the verses of the Quran!

Well, most likely, Muhammad feared that people would mix his words with the Quran. Not the primitive way that is depicted by the Sunnis and Shiites, since as we pointed out, there were many ways to eliminate that concern. But the real concern was different. Because of the warnings of the Quran, he had all the reasons to fear that Muslims would follow the footsteps of Jews and would create their own Mishna, Gomorra, and Talmud: *hadith* would be considered as an authority, as another source besides the Quran, setting him as partner with God! Ironically, the followers of *hadith* and *sunna* accomplished exactly that. They did not need to publish the text of *hadith* together with the Quran--though they have done that in many commentaries--they have been doing worse. Though they usually have kept *hadith* separate from the Quran physically, as far as for the purpose of guidance and religious authority, they mix it with the Quran. Even worse, they make the understanding of the Quran dependant to the understanding of *hadith*, thereby elevating *hadith* to position of authority over the Quran. Thus, if indeed Muhammad was worried about people mixing his words with the Quran, the followers of *hadith* proved his worries right: centuries after him, they did not only mix his words with the Quran, they mixed thousands of fabrication and nonsense attributed to him. See 25:30; 59:7.

8. Give me one, only one "*hadith*" that you think is necessary for my salvation besides the Quran. If you are not ready to discuss the necessity and accuracy of a single *hadith*, then please give inviting people to *hadith* and *Sunna*.

Further Discussion

Sunni: The bound collection of testimony from any court is certain to contain some lies and some errors. The reliability of any piece of evidence remains debatable. Where the narrators agree, where there is no irreconcilable conflict with the Quran, where the *hadith* is not offensive to *tawhid*, etc., we may well be justified in accepting it as reliable. And if a collector collects a thousand *hadith* and makes a few errors, neither is he to be condemned as unreliable.

Muslim: Not a single court will accept the testimony of Bukhari who collected contradictory *hadith*s about the Prophet Muhammad, narrated from generation to generation 200 years after his departure. You try to minimize the number and size of errors. There are hundreds of lies, not "a few errors." And they are grave ones. They attribute silly and contradictory laws and words to God. They create a manmade religion in the name of God! They are full of insult to God and his messenger. They are not trivial, since God Almighty does not accept those "few errors" as trivial:

" . . . Who is more evil than the one who fabricates lies and attributes them to God?" (29:68)

Sunni: If the *hadith* are not *mutawatir*, the monotheist Muslim should know by now that most scholars would say that one is free to disregard it, though not necessarily without peril. The issue the Muslim raises about the difficulties of decision regarding *hadith* also apply to personal interpretation of the Quran. No, the Quran makes it clear, we cannot disregard any evidence out of hand, not even the evidence of an unrighteous man; how much less the evidence of those against whom we have no evidence of unrighteousness or lack of caution?

Muslim: First, can you please tell us how many *mutawatir* (accepted with consensus) *Hadith* are there. What are they and where are they? Second, can you give me a few names of those "most scholars" who would say that I am free to disregard non-*mutawatir hadith*s? As far as for evidences.... Sure, we cannot disregard evidences for our daily affair, even of an unrighteous man. But, God's system is not left to the mercy of those evidences. God explained and sufficiently detailed his system in his book, which is described as complete, detailed, and perfect. It does not contain any doubt. Furthermore, God promised to preserve it. And He did it with a unique mathematical system which hypocrites and disbelievers are unable to see.

Sunni: I have answered The Muslim about of a number of these *hadith*. Certainly, I personally have trouble with certain *hadith*; however, I must always ask myself whether or not it is my own view which is in error, rather than the *hadith*. Perhaps there is something I have not thought of.

For example, there is a *hadith*, which The Muslim loves to cite mentioning the drinking of camel's urine, which he seems to believe, is particularly ridiculous. Does he base this on a scientific study of the virtues of drinking camel's urine? I think not. Nor does he ever mention that nomadic peoples, not just Arabs but including them, often consume the waste products of their animals. So "cannot accept" is definitely culturally conditioned. But no one has claimed that drinking camels' urine is required of any Muslim.

Muslim: Well, prescribing camels' urine is the minor problem of that *hadith*. You can even find some Sunni doctors who pontificate that camel's urine is a panacea for every disease. The big problem was about gouging their eyes after pruning all their legs and hands, etc. You craftily skipped that part.

Sunni: The Muslim confuses *Hadith* and *Sunna*. *Hadith* is only one of a number of major sources of *Sunna*, other major sources being the Qur'an and the practice of the community. The latter is how we generally learn to pray, by the way. To answer the question about necessity of *hadith* without going deeply into the whole concept of necessity is impossible.

But I will answer this way: if a *hadith* transmits a wisdom necessary in a particular situation, and one turns away from that wisdom merely because it was

94

a *hadith* (and not some other preferred modality), then one becomes culpable for failure to act correctly in the situation. This could, indeed lead to hell-fire. Of course, the same is true of the Qur'an, or even the preaching of a Christian.

Muslim: If you think that some one is wrong and even misguided because of his rejection of *hadith* and that person challenges you with that question you don't answer like you did above. You did not or could not answer my challenge. Answering questions is not an act of writing irrelevant lines after the question. Please come to the point.

A Revolution Led by a Gentile against the Mollarchy of Medieval Arabia[1]

It was 570 years after Christ when Muhammad was born in Mecca. At age 40 he made a declaration that shocked his people. During the month of Ramadan of 610, he claimed that he was visited by Holy Revelation (a.k.a. Jibreel or Holy Spirit) delivering him a message from God. This claim was first kept secret he shared only with several close friends and relatives. A few years later he publicly declared his messengership and his opposition to the religious and political establishment of Mecca. An era of revolution and reformation that would change world history had started.

Muhammad, a member of a powerful tribe and a successful international businessman, was not an ordinary citizen of Mecca. With his sound judgment and trustworthy personality, he had won the respect of the theocratic oligarchy. His uncles were the leaders of one of the prominent tribes and were active in social, political, economic and religious affairs.

Arabs living in the Hijaz region were brethren of Jews, and Abraham was their common forefather. Mecca or Bacca was the valley where Abraham had immigrated, after his exile from Babylon. There is only one reference to this important city in the Old Testament:

> Blessed is the man whose strengths in thee; in whose heart are the ways of them. Who passing through the valley of **Baca** make it a well; the rain also fills the pools. They go from strength to strength, every one of them in Zion appears before God. O LORD God of hosts, hear my prayer: give ear, O God of Jacob. (Psalms 84:5-8)

Meccan Arabs had deep respect to the struggle of Abraham whose courageous stand for his monotheistic belief was a legend. Therefore, they were very protective of his reputation, religious practices, and the Kaba. Knowing that Abraham rejected worshiping the statutes besides God, Arabs never worshiped statutes, or symbolic objects.[2] Nevertheless, they had holy names, such as Al-lat,

---

[1] From the introductory section of Edip Yuksel's upcoming book, NINETEEN: God's Signature in Scripture and Nature.

[2] The common belief among Muslims is to the contrary. Clerics and scholars, in order to distinguish themselves from the Meccan mushriks, fabricated stories about statues. There are dubious narrations that Muhammad broke statutes occupying Kaba. However, the Quran that occasionally refers to the statues of previous communities (see: 6:74; 7:138; 14:35; 21:57; 26:71),never mentions the statues or icons of Meccan mushriks. Furthermore, there is no archeological evidence to support the claims of

Al-Uzza, and Manat from whom they would ask intercession and help. Their association of other authorities and powers to God and their fabrication of myriad prohibitions and laws in the name of God is called *shirk*[3] and the Quran repeatedly criticizes this mindset and practice as polytheism, the source of all evil.

> What do you think about Allat (The Goddess), Al-Uzza? And Manat, the third one. Do you have sons, while He has daughters? What a fraudulent distribution! These are but names that you made up, you and your forefathers. God never authorized such a blasphemy. They follow conjecture, and personal desire, when the true guidance has come to them herein from their Lord. What is that the human being desires? To God belongs both the Hereafter, and this world. Not even the angels in heaven possess authority to intercede. The only ones permitted by God are those who act in accordance with His will and His approval. (53:19-26)

> Have they have invented intercessors to mediate between them and God? Say, "What if they do not possess any power, nor understanding?" Say, "All intercession belongs to God." To Him belongs the kingship of the heavens and the earth, then to Him you will be returned. When God alone is mentioned, the hearts of those who do not acknowledge in the Hereafter shrink with aversion. But when others are mentioned besides Him, they rejoice. (39:43-45).

However, those who accepted other authorities besides God, never accept their crime. They vehemently deny their *shirk*. Though majority of "believers" follow the teachings of their clergymen and assign divine authority to others besides God, they usually do not accept that they are committing *shirk*; they claim to be monotheists. If you question a Hindu who worships hundreds of gods and goddesses, you will learn that he or she is really a monotheist! A Christian who puts his full confidence in St. Paul's polytheistic teaching which was formulated 325 AC by the Nicene Council as the Doctrine of Trinity (i.e., God with three personalities) will still claim to be a monotheist![4] Muslims who elevated Muhammad to the level of God by making him the second source of their

---

Muslim scholars. Besides, the classic book about statues, Al-Kalbi's KITAB UL ASNAM (The Book of Statues), contains many contradictory descriptions of the so-called Arabian statues. Muslim historians who were disturbed by lack of material evidence for the allegedly abundant Arabian statues came up with a "cookie" theory: Meccan idol-worshipers were making their statues from cookies and when they got hungry they used to eat them. That should explain why archeologist cannot find statues in the region for that era! Phew!

[3] Shirk is described by the Quran in various contexts. Setting up partners with God, or accepting prophets, clergymen and scholars as **authorities** in God's religion is considered as an unforgivable sin. See 42:21; 9:31; 3:18; 2:48; 6:21; 6:145; 7:17-37; 17:46; 45:6; 16:89; 6:112-115; 19:82; 46:6; 25:30; etc.

[4] See the author's book, "19 Questions For Christian Clergy."

religion and by putting his name next to God in the Statement of Testimony, will also insist that they are monotheists.

> On the day when we summon everyone, we will ask the mushriks, "Where are those whom you claimed partners?" Their only response will be, "By God our Lord, we never were mushriks." (6:22-23)

> Those who commit shirk say, "Had God willed, we would not have worshiped anyone besides Him, nor would our parents. Nor would we have prohibited anything besides (what was prohibited by) Him." Those before them have done the same. Can the messengers do anything but deliver the message? (16:35)

Arab mushriks (those who accept other authorities besides God) never claimed that those holy names were gods, they were merely praying for their intercession. They believed that the saints and angles were mediators between them and God.

> Absolutely, the system shall be devoted to God ALONE. Those who set up masters besides Him say, "We worship them only to bring us closer to God; they are in a good position!" God will judge them regarding their disputes. God does not guide any liar, unappreciative. (39:3)

The Quran clearly rejects association of any authority besides God, whether in making the religious laws or providing eternal salvation.

> They follow those who decree for them religious laws never authorized by God. If it were not for the predetermined decision, they would have been judged immediately. Indeed, the transgressors have incurred a painful retribution. (42:21)

> They have set up their religious leaders and scholars as lords, instead of God. Others deified the Messiah, son of Mary. They were all commanded to worship only one God. There is no God except He. Be He glorified, high above having any partners. (9:31)

According to the information given by the Quran, Meccan Mushriks preserved the forms of religious practices while they lost its monotheistic and spiritual meaning. They were praying, fasting, and going to pilgrimage.[5] It was the most popular religious practice.

Mollarchy in the City State of the Arabian Peninsula

There were some characteristics of Mecca that distinguished it from other Arabian towns and cities. Mecca, with the Abraham's temple, was the center of religion, politics and business. Abraham's temple, the Kaba, is described by the

---

[5]   The detailed argument on this subject can be found in author's Turkish book, "Errors in the Translations of the Quran."

98

Quran as "People's House" or "Sacred Place of Prostration." Abraham, as I mentioned above, was a legendary ancestor for both Arabs and Jews. During the four consecutive sacred months,6 Arabs dwelling in the region would visit Mecca for pilgrimage. Meanwhile, the occasion was also used for an international trade fair. Merchants from neighboring countries would participate in a lengthy business and cultural activity. During these religious months, besides trading, cultural and athletic competitions such as poetry, competition, and wrestling would take place. Mecca was the center of economic, political, and cultural activities of a vast land.

Prominent tribal leaders like Abu Hakem (a.k.a., Abu Jahel), Abdul Uzza (a.k.a., Abu Lahab), Abu Sufyan, Umayy Ben Halef, Nadr Ben Haris, and Valeed Ben Mugiyra, could not tolerate any reformation movement that would change the status quo and risk Mecca's crucial position in political and economic landscape. They were determined to follow the traditional religion they inherited from their ancestors who had distorted Abraham's monotheistic system to shirk. Preservation of the traditional religion and the status quo was vital for the theocratic government of Mecca. Questioning the orthodox belief system and the common practice could be interpreted as a foreign attack to the unity or as a betrayal to the fabric of the society.

A teaching that rejects the idea of intercession and the sacred role of professional clergymen, a teaching that promotes the human rights of slaves and the oppressed, that seeks economic justice by objecting monopoly and usury, that is concerned about the poor, that condemns ethnic and racial discrimination, that protects the rights of women, that advocates democratic governance through consultation, and encourages people to use their reasoning and questions the tradition, surely, such a system would pose a serious threat to the economic and political interest of the ruling elite.

Social, economic, and political structure criticized

It is a well-known fact that the early revelations of the Quran use a strong language in criticizing the theocratic oligarchy, which did not care about the poor, orphans and aliens; did not free the slaves; did not treat women equal to men; and did not consult people in public affairs.

> Do you know who rejects The System of God Alone? That is the one who mistreats the orphans. And does not advocate the feeding of the poor. And woe to those who observe the contact prayers, Who are totally heedless of their prayers; they only show off. And they forbid charity. (107:1-7).

> Wrong! It is you who brought it on yourselves by not regarding the orphan. And not advocating charity towards the poor. And consuming

---

6   They were originally Zilhija, Muharram, Safar, Rabi 1, and later their order was changed by mushriks.

the inheritance of helpless orphans. And loving the money too much. (89:17-20).

He boasts, "I spent so much money!" Does he think that no one sees him? Did we not give him two eyes? A tongue and two lips? Did we not show him the two paths? He should choose the difficult path. Which one is the difficult path? The freeing of slaves. Feeding, during the time of hardship. Orphans who are related. Or the poor who is in need. And being one of those who acknowledge, and exhorting one another to be steadfast, and exhorting one another to be kind. These have deserved happiness. As for those who did not acknowledge our revelations, they have incurred misery. They will be confined in the Hellfire. (90:6-20).

Thus, when one of them gets a baby girl, his face becomes darkened with overwhelming grief. Ashamed, he hides from the people, because of the bad news. He even debates: should he keep the baby grudgingly, or bury her in the dust. Miserable indeed is their judgment. (16:58-59).

And they respond to their Lord by observing the contact prayers and by deciding their affairs on the basis of consultation among themselves, and from our provisions to them they give (42:38).

O people, observe your Lord; the one who created you from one being and created from it its mate, then spread from the two many men and women. You shall regard God, by whom you swear, and regard the parents. God is watching over you. You shall hand over to the orphans their rightful properties. Do not substitute the bad for the good, nor shall you consume their properties by combining them with your properties. This is a gross injustice. If you deem it best for the orphans, you may marry their mothers –you may marry two, three, or four of them. If you fear lest you become unfair, then you shall be content with only one, or with what you already have. This way, you are more likely to avoid inequity. You shall give the women their due dowries, fully. If they willingly forfeit anything, then you may accept it graciously. Do not give immature orphans the properties that God has entrusted you as guardians. You shall provide for them therefrom, and clothe them, and talk to them nicely. (4:1-5)[7]

---

[7] The purpose and practice of polygamy is another distorted issue in islam (submission). Though the Quran discourage polygamy with two verses (4:3 and 4:129), it allows it as a social and economic institution to take care of orphans in a family environment. The Quran allows polygamy with widows who have children. This permission allowed those who could afford to marry with widows to provide a father figure to their children and take care of their needs. Interestingly, the verse clarifying this limited permission is traditionally mistranslated despite its clear grammatical structure. The correct translation of the verse:

Whatever God restored to His messenger from the (defeated) communities shall go to God and His messenger (in the form of a charity). You shall give it to the relatives, the orphans, the poor, and the traveling alien. Thus, it will not remain monopolized by the strong among you. You may keep the spoils given to you by the messenger, but do not take what he enjoins you from taking. You shall reverence God. God is strict in enforcing retribution. (59:7)

Life Style and Harmful Tradition Criticized

The population of Mecca was afflicted with many social problems caused by individual abuses of time, money, brain, body, and exploitation of God's name.

For instance, gambling was transferring money from the poor to the wealthy, thereby creating financial nightmares for many families. Alcohol was the cause of many personal and social problems such as domestic violence, inefficiency, loss of intellectual capabilities, alcoholism, rape, criminal activities, accidents and myriad of health problems. The Quran, though acknowledged some financial and personal benefits of gambling and alcohol, encouraged muslims to abstain from these addictions without criminalizing them via penal code.

> They ask you about intoxicants and gambling: say, "In them there is a gross sin, and some benefits for the people. But their sinfulness far outweighs their benefit." They also ask you what to give to charity: say, "The excess." God thus clarifies the revelations for you, that you may reflect. (2:219)

> O you who acknowledge, do not observe the Contact Prayers (Salat) while intoxicated, so that you know what you are saying.... (4:43)

> O you who acknowledge, intoxicants, and gambling, and the altars of idols, and the games of chance are abominations of the devil; you shall avoid them, that you may succeed.(5:90)

> And from the fruits of date palms and grapes you produce intoxicants, as well as good provisions. This should be (sufficient) proof for people who understand. (16:67)

Sexual promiscuity or adultery was contributing in the destruction of families and was a major health threat for public by transmitting sexual diseases. The

---

"They consult you concerning women: say, 'As recited for you in the scripture, God enlightens you regarding the rights of orphans of women whom you deprive of their dowries while seeking to marry them, regarding the disadvantaged children: you shall treat the orphans equitably. Whatever good you do, God is fully aware thereof." (4:127).
Unfortunately, Muslim Scholars abused this limited permission and justified marrying with four women at a time even without the permission of the first wife who was deprived her right to divorce!

Quran encouraged men and women to be loyal to their marriage contract. Though polygamy is permitted to take care of fatherless children and their widowed mothers, monogamy was encouraged.

> You shall not commit adultery; it is a gross sin, and an evil behavior. (17:32)

> If you deem it best for the orphans, you may marry their mothers - you may marry two, three, or four. If you fear lest you become unfair, then you shall be content with only one, or with what you already have. Additionally, you are thus more likely to avoid financial hardship.(4:3)

Lengthy list of dietary prohibitions concocted in the name of God was wasting many food resources. The Quran prohibited only four items related to animal products and considered any additional religious prohibitions to be fabrications and shirk.

> Say, "I do not find in the revelations given to me any food that is prohibited for any eater except: (1) carrion[8], (2) running blood, (3) the meat of pigs, for it is bad,[9] and (4) the meat of animals blasphemously dedicated to other than God." If one is forced (to eat these), without being deliberate or malicious, then your Lord is Forgiver, Most Merciful. For those who are Jewish we prohibited animals with undivided hoofs; and of the cattle and sheep we prohibited the fat, except that which is carried on their backs, or in the viscera, or mixed with bones. That was a retribution for their transgressions, and we are truthful. If they do not acknowledge you, then say, "Your Lord possesses infinite mercy, but His retribution is unavoidable for the guilty people." The idol worshipers say, "Had God willed, we would not practice idolatry, nor would our parents, nor would we prohibit anything." Thus did those before them did not acknowledge, until they incurred our retribution. Say, "Do you have any proven knowledge that you can show us? You follow nothing but conjecture; you only guess." Say, "God possesses the most powerful argument; if He wills He can guide all of you." Say, "Bring your witnesses who would testify that God has prohibited this or that." If they testify, do not testify with them. Nor shall you follow the opinions of those who reject our revelations, and those who do not acknowledge in the Hereafter, and those who

---

[8]   The examples of this category are listed in verse 5:3.

[9]   Many speculations made by Muslims to provide medical reasons for prohibition of *meat* of pig. Though, I consider it as a divine commandment to be followed for just the sake of obeying the Creator of the Universe, I think one of the reasons might lay in the waste of resources and environmental pollution. It is a well-known fact that pigs produce 6 times more waste than other domestic animals. Pig farms have caused serious environmental problems in some States, such as in North Carolina. Besides emitting disturbing smell, pig waste has contaminated the underground water in many nearby towns.

stray away from their Lord. Say, "Come let me tell you what your Lord has really prohibited for you: You shall not set up idols besides Him. You shall honor your parents. You shall not kill your children from fear of poverty - we provide for you and for them. You shall not commit gross sins, obvious or hidden. You shall not kill - God has made a person's life sacred - except in the course of justice. These are His commandments to you, that you may understand." (6:145-151)

The Quran dealt with many other issues such as protection of environment and ecological balance and protection of God's creation from unnecessary mutilation. For instance, the Quran prohibited hunting during pilgrimage (5:95-96). It also criticized Meccan Arabs for cutting the ears of animals for religious reasons, which has negative implication regarding the custom of circumcision.

"I will mislead them, I will entice them, I will command them to (forbid the eating of certain meats by) marking the ears of livestock, and I will command them to distort the creation of God." Anyone who accepts the devil as a lord, instead of God, has incurred a profound loss. (4:119)

The chapter "Ben Israel" (Children of Israel) contains a series of commandments aiming to change the mindset, attitude and actions of individuals:

You shall not set up any other God beside God, lest you end up despised and disgraced. Your Lord has decreed that you shall not worship except Him, and your parents shall be honored. As long as one or both of them live, you shall never say to them, "Uff" (the slightest gesture of annoyance), nor shall you shout at them; you shall treat them amicably. And lower for them the wings of humility, and kindness, and say, "My Lord, have mercy on them, for they have raised me from infancy." Your Lord is fully aware of your innermost thoughts. If you maintain righteousness, He is Forgiver of those who repent. You shall give the due alms to the relatives, the needy, the poor, and the traveling alien, but do not be excessive, extravagant. The extravagant are brethren of the devils, and the devil is unappreciative of his Lord. Even if you have to turn away from them, as you pursue the mercy of your Lord, you shall treat them in the nicest manner. You shall not keep your hand stingily tied to your neck, nor shall you foolishly open it up, lest you end up blamed and sorry. For your Lord increases the provision for anyone He chooses, and reduces it. He is fully Cognizant of His creatures, Seer. You shall not kill your children (infanticide) due to fear of poverty. We provide for them, as well as for you. Killing them is a gross offense. You shall not commit adultery; it is a gross sin, and an evil behavior. You shall not kill any person - for God has made a person's life sacred - except in the course of justice. If one is killed unjustly, then we give his heir authority to enforce justice. Thus, he shall not exceed the limits in avenging the murder; he will be helped. You shall not touch the orphans' money except for their own good, until they reach maturity. You shall fulfill your covenants, for a covenant is a great responsibility. You shall give full measure when you trade, and weigh equitably. This is better and more righteous. You shall not accept any information, unless you verify it for yourself. I have given you the hearing, the eyesight, and the brain, and you are responsible for using them. You shall not walk proudly on earth - you cannot bore through the earth, nor can you be as tall as the mountains. All bad behavior is condemned by your Lord. This is some of the wisdom inspired to you by your Lord. You shall not set up another God beside God, lest you end up in Gehenna, blamed and defeated. (17:23-39)

The Quran aimed to reform both the society and the individual. The Quran invites individuals to undertake a substantial reformation. The description of the acknowledgers in the last verses of chapter "Al-Furqan" (The Distinguisher) reveals the desired characteristics of muslims:

You shall put your trust in the One who is Alive - the One who never dies - and praise Him and glorify Him. He is fully Cognizant of His creatures' sins. He is the One who created the heavens and the earth, and everything between them, in six days, then assumed all authority. The Gracious; ask about Him those who are well founded in knowledge. When they are told, "Fall prostrate before the Gracious," they say, "What is the Gracious? Shall we prostrate before what you advocate?" Thus, it only augments their aversion. Most blessed is the One who placed constellations in the sky, and placed in it a lamp, and a shining moon. He is the One who designed the night and the day to alternate: a sufficient proof for those who wish to take heed, or to be appreciative. The worshipers of the Gracious are those who tread the earth gently, and when the ignorant speak to them, they only utter peace. In the privacy of the night, they meditate on their Lord, and fall prostrate. And they say, "Our Lord, spare us the agony of Hell; its retribution is horrendous. "It is the worst abode; the worst destiny." When they give, they are neither extravagant nor stingy; they give in moderation. They never implore beside God any other God, nor do they kill anyone - for God has made life sacred - except in the course of justice. Nor do they commit adultery. Those who commit these offenses will have to pay. Retribution is doubled for them on the Day of Resurrection, and they abide therein humiliated. Exempted are those who repent, acknowledge, and lead a righteous life. God transforms their sins into credits. God is Forgiver, Most Merciful. Those who repent and lead a righteous life, God redeems them; a complete redemption. They do not bear false witness. When they encounter vain talk, they ignore it. When reminded of their Lord's revelations, they never react to them as if they were deaf and blind. And they say, "Our Lord, let our spouses and children be a source of joy for us, and keep us in the forefront of the righteous." These are the ones who attain Paradise in return for their steadfastness; they are received therein with joyous greetings and peace. Eternally they abide therein; what a beautiful destiny; what a beautiful abode. Say, "You attain value at my Lord only through your worship. But if you do not acknowledge, you incur the inevitable consequences." (25:58-77)

Meccan Leaders are Losing Their Sleep

Mecca could remain an independent center of commerce because of its unique geopolitical situation. Mecca was located in a region where the influence of the two super powers of the era, Byzantine and Persian Empires, collided. This balance of powers created such a vacuum that Mecca could survive without submitting herself to either hegemony. Mecca was a default capital of the Arabian Peninsula. The population of Mecca and surrounding towns did not follow any scripture, but only oral traditions and practices. Religion and politics were inseparable affairs. Though Meccan population had many literate people, they were considered "UMMY" (gentiles) for not having a scripture or a written law like their Christian and Jewish neighbors. Muhammad was a literate gentile.[10]

When Muhammad declared that he received a message from God, the Meccan oligarchy first did not take him seriously. They just ignored him. However, when they noticed the potential power of his message and the rate of the new converts, their reaction varied between mockery and insinuation. Soon their reaction escalated to slander and threat of eviction and death. Though Muhammad's personal history and his tribal relationship was providing a kind of protection against physical attacks, some of his followers did not have tribal support. For instance, among those who were subjected to torture was Bilal, an Ethiopian slave who was freed by one of Muhammad's friend. The first

---

[10] Muslim scholars, among many facts, have distorted this one too. They fabricated and narrated stories claiming that Muhammad was an illiterate man and maintained his illiteracy until his death. This claim not only contradicts the Quran and the historical facts, but it is also an insult to Muhammad. Was the prophet who brought a book and dictated it for 23 years not able to recognize the 28 letters of Arabic alphabet? How come a prophet who brought a scripture, which its first revelation starts with the word "READ," did not try to learn how to read? Why a prophet who encouraged his friends to learn how to read and write himself did not practice what he preached to others? If Muhammad was illiterate, then he was either a crook trying to fool people that he could not read (which is impossible since there were literally thousands of people who knew him since his childhood) or he did not have the intelligence to learn how to read and write! To support their claim of "Literal Miracle" Muslim Scholars resorted to this obvious lie and interestingly reached consensus on it! For a detailed argument on this, please see the Introduction of Quran: a Reformist Translation.

105

convert[11] who was killed was Sumayya, a woman. Slaves and women. Victims of racist and misogynistic laws and religions.

Clergymen who had economic and political interest in their corrupt religious teachings, augmented and manipulated the religious fanaticism of ignorant masses. The fatal combination of ignorance and arrogance, which in the past had taken the lives of many messengers and prophets, from Socrates to Jesus, was again at work. The words uttered against previous messengers were repeated against Muhammad, this time in Arabic. Muhammad's situation was no different than Saaleh, a messenger to a community perished long time ago.

> They said, "O Saaleh, you used to be popular among us before this. Are you enjoining us from worshiping what our parents are worshiping? We have a lot of doubt concerning everything you tell us. (11:62)

Muhammad's message was focused on monotheism (tawheed), which is the main theme of Mosaic teaching that crowns the Ten Commandments.

> And God spoke all these words, saying, I am the LORD thy God, which have brought you out of the land of Egypt, out of the house of bondage. Thou shall have no other gods before me. Thou shall not make unto thee any graven image, or any likeness of any thing that is in heaven above, or that is in the earth beneath, or that is in the water under the earth.... Thou shall not take the name of the LORD thy God in vain; for the LORD will not hold him guiltless that takes his name in vain. (Exodus 20:1-4, 7)

Ironically, despite the popularity of Ten Commandments among Jews, Christians and Muslims, the faith and practices negating and defying the first two commandments have become their basic dogmas.

Muhammad delivered the words of the Quran critical of the traditional religion of Meccan people who had transformed Abraham's monotheistic system to polytheism by blindly following their ancestors, inheriting innovations, superstitions, numerous cleric-made religious laws falsely attributed to God, and the belief of intercession.

> Say, "My Lord has guided me in a straight path: the perfect system of Abraham, monotheism. He never was an idol worshiper." (6:161)

Flocking on the Glorious Path of their Ancestors

Mushriks, be it of ancient times or modern times, attempt to justify their religions by the number of their members, by the glory of their ancestors and by the fame of their "saints." In arguments based on logic, scientific investigation and analysis of historical documentation, their common defense is the miserable

---

[11] Meccan Arabs initially called Muhammad and his followers, "Sabeen" meaning "followers of other religions."

argument from authority: "this and that holy clergymen said this," or "most of our ancient scholars have decided this way."

> Instead, they said, "We found our parents carrying on certain practices, and we are following in their footsteps. Invariably, when we sent a warner to a community, the leaders therein said, "We found our parents following certain practices, and we will continue in their footsteps." He would say, "What if I brought to you better guidance than what you inherited from your parents?" They would say, "We are reject in the message you brought." (43:22-24).

> When they are told, "Follow these revelations of God," they say, "No, we follow only what we found our parents doing." What if the devil is leading them to the agony of Hell? Those who submit completely to God, while leading a righteous life, have gotten hold of the strongest bond. For God is in full control of all things. (31:21-22)

Idolizing their ancestors under different titles and following the dogmas and superstitions that are attributed to them as a religion is the universal characteristics of mushriks. Religious idols vary according to religions and languages. For instance, idols, in America are Jesus, Mary or Saint; in Turkey are Ata, Evliya, Sheik or Hazrat; in India Mahatma; in Pakistan Maulana; in Iran Imam, Hussein and Ehl-i Bayt. Religious masses do not seek the truth by using their brains and senses. Instead, they blindly follow the teachings bearing sanctified signatures. Mushriks are like parrots; they repeat words without understanding their meaning.

> The example of those who do not acknowledge is like those who parrot what they hear of sounds and calls, without understanding. Deaf, dumb, and blind; they cannot understand. (2:171)

Ironically, it is the religious leaders who promote blind imitation. By institutionalizing ignorance via religious terms, the diabolic saints lead astray masses from Truth.[12] The messengers and prophets, who invited people to question their popular religion and traditions, almost invariably found the clergymen fighting and plotting against them.

---

[12] The famous atheist philosopher, Friedrich Nietzsche, was so fed up with the abuse and exploitation of the Church, he opened a scorching attack on clergymen. He wrote, "As long as the priest is considered a higher type of man—this professional negator, slanderer, and poisoner of life—there is no answer to the question: what is truth? For truth has been stood on its head when the conscious advocate of nothingness and negation is accepted as the representative of "truth." ... In Christianity neither morality nor religion has even a single point of contact with reality.... This world of pure fiction is vastly inferior to the world of dreams insofar as the latter mirrors reality, whereas the former falsifies, devalues, and negates reality. Friedrich Nietzsche, *The Antichrist*, in *The Portable Nietzsche*, ed. and trans. Walter Kaufmann (New York: Viking, 1954).

Nevertheless among the chief rulers also many acknowledged him; but because of the Pharisees they did not confess him, lest they should be put out of the synagogue: For they loved the praise of men more than the praise of God. (John 12:42-43)

The leaders announced, "Go and steadfastly persevere in worshiping your gods. This is all you need. We never heard of this from the religion of our fathers. This is a lie. Why did the message come down to him, instead of us?" Indeed, they are doubtful of My message. Indeed, they have not yet tasted My retribution. (38:6-8)

The Black Campaign Waged by Those with White Turbans

The message delivered by Muhammad baffled and bewildered the bearded and turbaned Meccan clerics. They first tried to attack his character. They accused and insulted him to be a "wizard," a dreaming "poet," or "a crazy man."

Do not set up besides God any other God. I am sent by Him to you as a manifest warner. Consistently, when a messenger went to the previous generations, they said, "Magician," or, "Crazy." Did they make an agreement with each other? Indeed, they are transgressors. (51:51-53)

When they were told "La Elaaha Ella Allah [There is no other God besides God]," they turned arrogant. They said, "Shall we leave our gods for the sake of a crazy poet?" (37:35-36)

Those who do not acknowledged show their ridicule in their eyes when they hear the message and say, "He is crazy!" It is in fact a message to the world. (68:51-52)

The Quran encourages Muhammad not to give up against this negative propaganda. Muhammad's mission was to deliver the message at the cost of losing his popularity.

You shall remind the people. With your Lord's blessings upon you, you are neither a soothsayer, nor crazy. They may say, "He is a poet; let us just wait until he is dead." Say, "Go on waiting; I will wait along with you." Is it their dreams that dictate their behavior, or are they naturally wicked? Do they say, "He made it all up?" Instead, they are simply ingrates. (52:29-33)

The Reaction and Plans of Ingrates

Tyranny and terror is a prevalent characteristic of mushriks. Terror and violence is a defense mechanism of many who prefer not to use their brains. The polytheistic elite of Athena convicted Socrates to death for questioning the absurdity of their religion. Persian priests tried to get rid of Zoroaster. Jewish clerics conspired with Romans to kill Jesus for his threat to their abuse of religion. In defense of his theocratic and oppressive regime, Pharaoh mobilized his generals and religious leaders to eliminate Moses. Shuayb's life was

108

threatened by his people. Noah was stoned. Abraham was rejected by his own father and was thrown to fire. Some messengers were evicted and others were killed. Muhammad, who declared intellectual war against slavery, subjugation of women, racism, superstitions, ignorance, illiteracy, ancestor-worship, and exploitation of religious beliefs, would not be treated differently.

> The ingrates plotted and schemed to naturalize you, or kill you, or banish you. However, they plot and scheme, but so does God. God is the best schemer. When our revelations are recited to them, they say, "We have heard. If we want to, we can say the same thing. These are only tales from the past." (8:30-31).

The forerunners who took all kinds of risks by siding with Muhammad, encountered difficult tests. They were excommunicated. They were rejected by their families and relatives. They experienced economic hardship. They were subjected to the insult and torture of mushrik Arabs. They were oppressed, banished from their land, and were viciously attacked. Many were killed; but they did not give up from their conviction and cause.

> The Arabs are the worst in unappreciation and hypocrisy, and the most likely to ignore the laws that God has revealed to His messenger. God is Omniscient, Most Wise. (9:97)[13]

Muhammad was the main target of mushrik Arabs. Not only he had lost his popularity among his people; his life was in danger. However, he was ordained by the Lord of the Universe. He was commissioned to deliver the Message without compromise. He became the recipient of the greatest possible honor, receiving revelation from God.

> ... God has sent down to you the scripture and wisdom, and He has thought you what you never knew. Indeed, God's blessing upon you have been great. (4:113)

While the multifarious aggressive campaign of the Meccan government and its allies in the region continued, Muhammad and his comrades promoted the freedom of expression and religious beliefs.

> Say, "O you ingrates. I do not worship what you worship. Nor do you worship what I worship. Nor will I ever worship what you worship. Nor will you ever worship what I worship. To you is your system, and to me is my system." (109:1-6)

The leaders whose political and economic interest was at risk, and the ignorant followers, whose conformity was disturbed, responded this message of "leave us alone" with violence. But, their bloody terror and noise could not prevent the light from piercing and destroying the layers of darkness.

---

[13] The following verse, 9:99, makes an exception of this statement.

Adventures of an Islamic Reformer at Oxford, London, and Istanbul

Edip Yuksel

To publicly discuss my recent book, <u>Manifesto for Islamic Reform</u>, I was invited to give four lectures in November 3-10, 2008. The topics were: A Manifesto for Islamic Reform, and Why Quran Alone through Reason:

> MECO, Oxford University, November 3.
> MECO, Oxford University, November 4.
> The Muslim Institute, London, November 5.
> TUYAP Book Fair, Istanbul, November 8.

Prof Taj Hargey, the founder of MECO (Muslim Educational Center of Oxford), picked me up from the airport with an old diesel Volkswagen. I had picked the wrong airport and thus he had to drive more than two hours in a heavy traffic to pick me up. Like all bloody Britons[1], he drove on the wrong side of the road, which made me experience constant anticipation of an imminent bloody traffic accident. Though Taj is a scholar in a prestigious school, he is not a stereotypical one. To my delight, I found him not be a pretentious snob living in ivory towers; he was a humble and a committed activist, a veteran who had tasted victory against the apartheid regime during his years in South Africa. His dedication to the message of rational monotheism or islam appeared to be exemplary. He is both a general and a soldier; a professor and a student; a leader and comrade. Almost single-handedly, with a shoe-string budget, he is putting a good fight against the powerful forces of Sunni and Shiite establishment, and at the same time fighting against the aggression of the British government. Forces of corruption from Saudi, Iran and Pakistan are spending hundreds of millions of pounds to keep the Muslim minority ignorant and backward. The bloody mullahs have interest in keeping the Muslim minority in ghettoes and Taj is struggling to create a British Muslim identity.

Taj told me that his organization lost about fifty percent of its membership for letting Prof. Amina Wadud lead the congregational prayer two weeks before my

---

[1]   As one of the principles I have committed myself since my childhood I never use cuss words, but somehow I do not find my habitual aversion against the British cussword "bloody". I am not exactly sure about its complete connotations and subtle innuendoes, but I am going to use it in this article as a British souvenir.

arrival. Though I find inconsistencies in Amina Wadud's theological position, she is a brave sister who is reminding Sunni and Shiite population the Quranic verse 49:13, a universal maxim of their holy book, which they have abandoned for the sake of fabricated teachings called *hadith* and *sunna*.

As it seems, a woman leading the prayer was the last straw on *mullah's* back; they unanimously excommunicated Taj and his organization. I was happy to learn that Taj was not naïve about the regressive powers against the reform movement and he was even more determined to fight against misogynistic mullahs. While he was hosting me, he was busy preparing for the upcoming annual music festival. Of course, music too is another divine blessing that mullahs prohibit. Imagine a singing muslim woman in front of men! Music + woman + spotlight! That would be a triple nightmare for them and Taj was going to organize it with an international flavor. Kill those self-righteous hair-splitting mullahs with beauty and music!

Multiple Choice Test or Theological Acid Test

My first lecture at Oxford University was received very well. We had productive discussions. A graduate student argued for historicity, that is, reading and usually limiting the Quran with its historic context. His friend criticized our reliance on science in understanding the Quranic verses. Citing a few abuses of such an approach, she wanted to refute any understanding of Quranic verses according to scientific facts. It took about ten minutes to show her the problems with her allergy against science and the problem with doubting proven mathematical statements. If there is any book on earth that should have complete compatibility with proven scientific facts and mathematics, it would be the books sent by the creator of the universe. I knew that their hidden distrust in Quran was the main factor in their rejection of science and mathematics. It is interesting that they employ impressive academic jargons to make such arguments.

I had prepared a test containing 45 multiple choice questions just the night before my travel. I duplicated them on both sides of a single sheet and I distributed to the audience before the lecture... They were asked to write their name, age, occupation, email address, favorite authors, and their sectarian affiliation. It was a bit awkward to test an audience that consisted of students and professors at one of the world's top universities. The multiple-choice test proved to be a powerful instrument to deliver the message of Islamic Reform under the light of the Quran. The correct answer for each multiple choice question was the E option, and for the Yes or No questions was the B option. So, it would take me a few seconds to evaluate the tests after they were returned to me.

The Sunni or Shiite test-takers found themselves in quagmire of contradiction with their own sectarian teachings. They learned that they were thirty, forty or even more than fifty percent infidels or heretics. Some of those who marked

Sunni as their sectarian affiliation contradicted the Sunni teachings on most of the issues. According to their own confessed sects, their lives were worthless; they deserved to be killed! I did not let this mirror or sect-o-meter remain an individual experience; I publicly declared the overall results. Many got all answers correct, including Eric, a monotheist from Unitarian church who already had a copy of the Quran: a Reformist Translation in his possession. Eric knew the original message of islam better than all the mullahs and the so-called "ulama" combined. And Eric was one of those muslims from among the People of the Book described by 2:62 and 74:31.

Let's Have Just One Percent Please, Just One Percent!

A Sunni professor who attended the lecture together with his wife could not handle the questions; he stopped after answering a few. It was amusing how during the discussion session he tried to bargain with me about the teachings of Hadith and Sunna. He realized that he could not defend most of the hadiths and sectarian teachings, so he begged for a compromise: "What about just 1% hadith?" I did not yield. I told him that we did not need to add even a tiny drop of coli bacteria into our food. Even one percent of shirk (partnership with God) is evil, and that one percent would mean that we still rejected God's repeated assertion that His book is detailed, complete, clarified and sufficient for guidance. Furthermore, that one percent hole in the book would be small; yet, it would allow insects, then mice and then get even bigger enough for a litter of pigs, perhaps bearded ones, to intrude. I reminded him that there was no difference between associating one partner or hundred partners to God.

The following night was the continuation of the previous lecture. I focused on the importance of critical thinking and using our God-given 19 rules of inference. I warned them against developing schizophrenic personalities, which almost all religious people do. I started with the following words:

Before putting anything in our mouths we observe the color, smell its odor. If it looks rotten or smells bad we do not touch it. If food passes the eye and nose tests, then our taste buds will be the judge. If a harmful bit fools all those examinations, our stomach come to rescue; it revolts and throws them up. There are many other organs that function as stations for testing, examination, and modification of imported material into our bodies. They ultimately meet our smart and vigilant nano-guards: white cells. Sure, there are many harmful or potentially harmful foods that pass all the way through our digestive system into our blood, such as alcohol and fat. Nevertheless, without using our reasoning faculty much if at all, we have an innate system that protects our body from harmful substances. It would be a mystery then how we can input information and assertions, especially the most bizarre ones, into our brains without subjecting them to the rigorous test of critical thinking. Our brains should never become trashcans of false ideas, holy viruses, unexamined dogmas and superstitions. We should be wise!

How can we protect our minds and brains? Do we have an innate system that protects us from harmful or junky ideas, especially dogmas or jingoisms that could turn us into zombies or self-righteous evil people? Yes we do: our logic is the program that detects and protects us against the most harmful viruses, which usually find their way when we are hypnotized by crowds, salespeople, politicians or clergymen.

The Prominent Imam with an Illiterate Role Model

For the third lecture, Taj took me to London. There I was going to give a lecture at Muslim Institute. I met some of familiar names, authors that I have known decades before, such as Dr. Ziyauddin Sardar and Dr. Ghayasudding Siddiqui. I also met some young reformers such as Farouk Peru, and Yusuf Desai and Nosheen Oezcan of Forward Thinking. I was positively surprised that with the exception of an imam there, who was considered a moderate and open minded one, they did not react in angry temper tantrums to my invitation to follow the Quran alone.

The imam rejected the Manifesto for Islamic Reform wholesale with a passionate opening. He accused me of distorting the facts. To substantiate his opposition, Imam Abduljalil Sajid picked one out of my assertions. He argued that Muhammad must have been illiterate. He did not provide an alternative take against my depiction of such illiteracy to be either an insult to Muhammad's intelligence or his intention. He did not bother to explain how a role model, a divinely selected messenger would not be able to recognize 28 Alphabet letters in 63 years of his life (two years for each letter!), or during the 23 years he received revelation that encouraged its audience to attain knowledge by reading. He did not deal with the problem of the alternative explanation, that is, how a role model could deliberately keep himself illiterate for all his life! Somehow, our imam, like all other religious leaders, had great tolerance for contradictions. His brain was filled with so many; he had perhaps given up from resolving them... A perfect example of intellectually boiled frog syndrome! I had empathy for him, since in my youth I was one of them. I let him vent his frustration.

Imam Abduljalil argued that the word *Iqra* did not mean read, but it meant recite. So, according to him, despite the instruction of verse 96:1, Muhammad could still have been illiterate. It was a late Monday night and we did not have time to engage in a lengthy discussion. For instance, I could remind him his own *hadith* which reported the first encounter of Muhammad and Angel Gabriel. According to that *hadith* report, when he was instructed with the first verse of chapter 96, *Iqra*, to make Muhammad read the visually displayed Quran, the angel squeezed him like a lemon several times when Muhammad claimed *"wa ma ana biqarin"* (I cannot read). Obviously that hadith report did not mean that Muhammad was incapable of repeating a word with two syllabi; it meant that he could not recognize the letters... He was contradiction with the hadith that was the basis for his assertion. I picked another argument.

-- Let's assume that you are right regarding the meaning of *Iqra*. Then, what is the Arabic word for "read"?

-- ???

-- Well, there must have been a word for reading in Arabic, since the Quran talks about books, about pen, about writing...

-- ???

Our imam who started his criticism with a loud denunciation suddenly turned mute. He could not even come up with a single word. I did not wish to push him further, since everyone in the room realized that he either did not know what he was arguing about or he realized that he was wrong. I remembered the most ridiculous praises in human history, where Muhammad is praised by millions for his illiteracy with the distorted meaning of the word "*ummy*" uttered together with another distorted word "*sally*". Thinking about the low illiteracy among the so-called Muslim population, I did not let the issue go away without a conclusive ending. I wanted to prove to him and everyone else that Muhammad was literate.

So, I used one of my successful teaching tools, which I employed first time in 1987 to convince Ali Bulaç, a prominent and prolific Muslim thinker who has numerous books and a Turkish Quran translation. After following my instructions, Ali was convinced in less than a minute that Muhammad must have been literate. Imagine the power of debunking the consensus of all Sunni and Shiite scholars in less than a minute! Imagine convincing a famous and popular Sunni author that all his Sunni scholars were wrong about an important issue. All in less than a minute! Yet, this proof has been implicitly provided in the Quran with the revelation of its first verses, through the very verses instructing how to read the Quran. What a marvelous book!

So, I tried that Quranic educational tool. I asked the imam to grab the pen and write down the beginning of chapter 96: "*Bismillahirrahmanirarrahim. Iqra bismi rabbika allazi khalaq*" That's it. Surprise: he did not wish to write it. Perhaps he was scared to continue engaging in a Socratic dialog. Had he written those few words, I would ask him why he wrote both words the same. Surely, he would be justified to spell them the same, since both were pronounced the same and meant the same. Then, I would ask him to look at the spelling of the Quran. He would notice that the one in *Bismillah* was consisted of three letters, BSM, but the one in the following verse was spelled with an extra aleph, BISM. So, even if we assume that Muhammad did not write the revelation of the Quran with his own hand, even if we believe in the stories of him dictating to scribes, he must have at least known the letter Aleph. If he knew Aleph, then he was at least 1/28th literate! "I proved that he knew the letter Aleph and now it is your turn to prove that he did not know the letter B, the second letter in alphabet," I would nicely ask. If our imam got stuck again, I would perhaps go forward and ask him about the different spelling of *Mecca* and *Becca* or the curious spelling of *Bastata* in verse 7:69.

I wanted to end the argument with the imam with an exposition. I knew his problem and I knew the fastest way to expose it. I told the audience that the gentleman was arguing about God's system without knowledge and without an enlightening book. I announced that I was going to prove that he did not in fact have respect for the Quran. I started reading from verse 6:145 and then posed him my question: "Do you have any other source or any other witness that adds more dietary prohibitions to the four items listed in this verse?" If he said no, he would contradict numerous hadiths and all sectarian teachings. If he said Yes, he would contradict this verse and would be exposed by the following verses as a "mushrik" (polytheist) for attributing the manmade religious prohibitions to God. He did not rush into saying Yes, as most of the Sunni scholars recklessly do. To my question regarding additional dietary prohibitions, he responded with extreme caution: "May be or may be not!" What? You are an "imam" in your fifties and you have eaten thousands of meals and you still do not know what is prohibited? And you are refuting the Quran alone for a "may be or may be not"? Do you exist? "Maybe or may be not?" Is eating shrimp *haram*? "Maybe or maybe not!" Is eating lobster *haram*? "Maybe or maybe not!" Are you okay? "Maybe or maybe not!"

For some of the audiences, that was the last straw that broke their already stressed respect for the imam. Several people got frustrated with him. One of them loudly yelled at him with animated arms: "If you do not know such a simple thing, then why are you debating with the guest speaker? Let him talk." Hearing his own people reprimanding him, the imam quietly left the room. I felt bad for him, but what he was doing was very wrong. He was trying to keep people in the darkness of ignorance. He was promoting shirk (polytheism) under the guise of monotheism. He was pretending to respect the prophet Muhammad while he was disrespecting the only book he delivered. He was insulting his intelligence by claming that he remained illiterate until his death. Yet, he insisted putting Muhammad's name next to God every time he uttered the monotheistic maxim. I hope that after hearing the message, he will show courage and wisdom to reject the fabricated Hadith and Sunna and uphold the Quran alone.

Detention at the Airport by the Turkish Police

The moment I arrived at the airport in Istanbul, I was immediately arrested by half a dozen young police officers who appeared to be celebrating the catch. After a boring day, they had a Turkish author (again) from the USA. I was informed about three charges against me, all involving political criticism of Turkish government and its policies. Some consisted of distortions of my published articles, exaggerations, or words taken out-of-context. And most did not even belong to me; they belonged to anonymous people who visit my websites and post their political opinions and criticism at the forums.

115

They took me to a nearby police station. When I entered the room, I noticed a poster filled with flags under the title: Independent Turkish Republics. Yes, in plural! I have no problem with such a sense of Turkish idealism. In fact, years ago, when the Turkish nations declared independence from Russia, I hoped and promoted an aggressive Turkish policy to create a unified block. Unfortunately, Turkey missed such an opportunity. However, when I heard the phone ring of an officer, I started getting a bit concerned. It was playing the Yeni Çeri march, "Ceddin deden, ceddin baban… hep kahraman Türk milleti…" (Your ancestors your grandparents, your ancestors your fathers… The Turkish nation has always been heroic…) At that point, I knew that I was among an openly racist police department. I have suffered from Turkish racism in many ways. For instance, my young brother Metin Yüksel, a legendary youth leader, was killed by Turkish fascists in 1979. I know first hand the evil of racism.

To my surprise and delight, the Turkish police was very kind and respectful. I am not sure how much of it was because of my American passport, but I think they had a radical change in attitude. They followed the legal procedure to the letter. They informed me about my right to stay silent, my right not to stay more than 24 hour in jail without going to the court. They were music to my ears; I felt as if I was dealing with a nice American police officer. The jail, which I spent the night, was very clean. I laid down on the floor, reading the Newsweek Magazine, a book on Evolution and Intelligent design, and Professor Stewart's Cabinet of Mathematical Curiosities. It was the best night ever I spent in a Turkish jail! Sure, this was a very low traffic police station and they could keep it cleaner than usual. Regardless, I could not believe in such a change, since it was very different from my experience with the Turkish police and jails years ago. During my heydays, in 1977-1987, I was a frequent host of those jails and they were horrible. Some would have raw sewer passing through, rats mingle with detainees, and when I get out, I would always get lice as souvenir. Compared to those Turkish jails, this one was like a five star hotel. I command the Turkish government for this great progress in respecting human dignity and rights.

Kurds, the Oppressed Minority

Well, I had also a bad experience, and should share that too. The chief of the police station treated me like a guest. He took me to his office and ordered food for me where I watched the Turkish TV for about an hour. This made me feel uncomfortable; I was kept unjustly yet I was feeling indebted to my captors. The weekly news program 32nd Day was on. The topic of the discussion was the chronic Kurdish problem. The panel had two Turkish politician or author. There was a good debate about the problem which was the making of the racist Turkish policy. The official racist ideology initially denied the existence of Kurds. Before 1970's, you could not find the word Kurds in the newspapers. The Turkish history text books still consider the Kurdish minority as non existent. Even the great Kurdish leader Salahaddin Ayyubi is described as a Turkish leader. Later, when denial became impossible, the racist Turkish oligarchy described them as Mountain Turks. They did not have a different language, there was no such a language called Kurdish.

Yet, they later shamelessly tried to ban the non-existent language and secured the ban of the language through an article in the Constitution of 1982, which was drafted by the generals who interrupted the young and fragile Turkish democracy, for the third time. The paranoid Turkish racism terrorized those Kurds who were politically active through contra-guerillas, mafia, and Gray Wolf fascists. They kidnapped, tortured and assassinated numerous Kurdish authors and leaders... In a journal article titled "Yes, I am a Kurd," I exposed the racist Turkish policy against Kurds. "My people are denied their identity, their culture, language, naming their own children, using their own land and living in freedom and security." (See: http://www.yuksel.org/e/law/kurd.htm) Kurds were even denied to celebrate their cultural holidays, such as, the Newroz (New Year). Its celebration was banned. When the racist policy politicized Kurds and led to the creation of various Kurdish political movements, including the terrorist PKK organization, the Turkish government was forced to recognize Newroz. Not as a Kurdish holiday, but a newly discovered ancient Turkish holiday! Since like religion, racism is capable of turning smart people into stupid people, they could not even think about the name of the holiday: The name of the officially hijacked Kurdish holiday was made of two Persian or Kurdish words: New (new) Roz (Day). In last decade, Kurds have received many rights, but with a huge cost, after losing the lives of tens of thousands and destruction of thousands of towns in South Eastern Turkey. The desire of Kurdish people for equality and dignity is still an ongoing struggle.

Back to the TV program... While listening to the panelists, the young police officer who had been treating me so nicely suddenly confessed: "If I did not have any expectation from life, I would get a machine gun and kill all of them." The other police officer, who was as young and nice, joined him by declaring his solution for the Kurdish problem: "We should just adopt the ways of our Ottoman ancestors; we should erect hundreds of stakes on the streets and hang hundreds of them on them. Then, you will not hear any Kurdish problem!" Now I knew why their phones were singing Ottoman military marches.

I did not raise objection. It would be futile to discuss with a group of racist police officers while they had me in their possession. Ignorance and arrogance feed each other, and they had plenty of both. Well, later I would be engaging in a Socratic dialogue with a bored nationalist police officer who stood by curiously asking some questions through the bars. Like most racists, he was in denial of his racism. But, all his arguments were biased and Turkish-centered. According to him, there was no problem in forcing Kurdish children to say "My existence should be a sacrificial to the existence of Turkishness" or "One Turk equals to the World," or "How happy is he who says 'I am a Turk'". Our discussion lasted about two hours until he was tired standing on his feet. I think,

I was able to penetrate his consciousness, showed him the mirror and placed major doubts in his mind about nationalism, which is one of the worst mental diseases of modern times.

Tried in two Continents in one Day

The Turkish police shuttled me between two courts, one in Asian the other in the European part of Istanbul, rushing to beat the deadline so that I would not stay in jail until the next Monday. I was not handcuffed during this travel; except briefly while I was taken to the car by a new police officer whom later was asked by his superior to unlock the handcuff.

I was also very impressed by the temperament of the judges and their just decision to release me and continue the court. When we arrived in Sultanahmet Adliyesi we rushed to the court's secretary's office. The judge happened to be sitting there. When he heard my name, he ordered the secretary that he knew where was the thick folder was. He pointed at one of the shelves on the wall. Indeed the folder was filled with papers, that is, copies of the hundreds of articles posted by hundreds of people at the forums of 19.org.

The judge initially worried me by telling me that he would continue the ban for my exit. But, he turned to be a very reasonable person. Perhaps he was just bluffing. Not knowing his intention I asked time for my attorney to come. The judge happily postponed the court to 2 pm afternoon. He read the illegal statements copied from my website's forums. They were primitive and colloquial insult words that I never use. I am puritan and I never use cuss words even in my privacy. They were, according to the complaint prosecutor, insulting Turkishness, insulting Turkish flag, insulting Turkish generals, insulting Turkish National Congress, insulting Turkish judges, insulting Turkish prosecutors, and insulting Turkish police officers. The prosecutor had agreed with the informant citizen that I had violated the article 301 of the Criminal Code and a few others. The charges were based on a complaint letter and supportive documents of a cult member affiliated to Adnan Oktar aka Harun Yahya, whose name was recognized by my attorney who has been defending the victims of this cult leader. (This cult leader has used the repressive Turkish laws to ban 19.org and many other popular sites, such as wordpress.com, youtube.com, and richarddawkins.net. Following his instructions, his followers are spamming the Internet with ugly false accusations against me.)

As later Taj would comfort me during my return to London, "if they did not accuse you of insulting Turkish pizza, Turkish bath, and Turkish coffee, no problem." Well, I had problem with the accusations. First, I would never insult Turkish race, since I am not a racist person. I believe that God allowed the children of Adam to diversify in color, culture and language in order to enrich our lives. I know that the superiority is not by color or ethnic group, but by righteous acts. Besides teaching philosophy at college, I was also teaching Turkish classes at my younger son's K-12 school in Arizona. According to the cultural attaché at the Turkish embassy in Washington, I was the first person in America that started teaching Turkish at a public K-12 school. I display a Turkish flag, its map, the picture of Mustafa Kamal Ataturk, and several beautiful pictures from Istanbul on the walls of the class I teach. Some parents traveled to Turkey just because of their children's exposure to Turkish language and culture. Perhaps, those who accused me of insulting Turkishness would never serve the interest of Turkish people as much as I have done. If I had wanted to retaliate against what the racist Turks had done to me and my family, perhaps I should have joined the ranks of PKK terror organization. I am a Kurd whose mother tongue was banned by the racist Turkish laws, whose brother was killed by Turkish nationalists, and who was imprisoned and tortured for four years for expressing opposing political views, and was forced to serve in Turkish military for 18 months as a "dangerous soldier."... As a rational monotheist, as a non-sectarian muslim, I could not have acted as my racist enemies. I promote unity and friendship between Kurds and Turks in all my writings on the issue.

I have written numerous articles critical of authoritarian generals who meddle with the Turkish democracy, or have written satires critical of flag-worshiper jingoists, or criticized the unjustified ban on women's headscarf, but they were never crude insults as they were stated. "Those words could not have written by me," I told the judge and the prosecutor on the bench. I was a skilled author and accusing me of authoring those primitive insults were in fact insult to my profession. "If I wished to insult those things," I said, "I could have insulted in style, in a much better language."

Though I find some of the Turkish laws suppressive of freedom of expression, I am very pleased that the legal system and police conduct have dramatically improved to the better. When it became clear that most of the "criminal words" did not belong to me, but belonged to the forum members at www.19.org , I was blamed for not censoring the postings of Turkish or Kurdish people who had expressed insults to Turkish government and national symbols.

The judge was a reasonable person and perhaps had problem with the article 301, which is now under consideration to be discarded. He dictated my statement, and instructed for my release and lifting the ban on my exit from Turkey. He wished to rule on the other two charges too, but they were not under his jurisdiction. We had to rush for the court at Kartal-Pendik region, on the Asian section of the city. We had less than an hour to beat the deadline of 5 pm. Otherwise I had to remain in jail until Monday, the day of my departure from Turkey. I would experience the fastest travel in Istanbul's heavy traffic. The police officers used the siren and zigzagged through the traffic, occasionally using the shoulder, made it to the court just seven minutes before 5 pm.

The middle-aged judge, while browsing my files, looked at me and asked me whether my brother was killed about thirty years ago. I was worried that he could be affiliated with the nationalists. Well, after asking me a few questions, he instructed my release. I am very thankful to the police officers who did their best to make my release possible by the end of the day. I had very little chance to get a release from the three charges.

The following day, I had a great reception at the book fair. This was my third real public appearance since my immigration to the USA, about 19 years ago. For security reasons, I had to limit my activities with TV programs that allowed me to encounter religious scholars through live debates. The lecture room was filled with enthusiastic audience. The reporter from the weekly Tempo magazine later told me about his impression. He was surprised to see a diverse demographics: young and old, men and women, women with headscarves and women wearing modern attire... They were very peaceful and friendly to my arguments.

During the remaining two days in Istanbul, I had an interview for Tempo Magazine's upcoming cover story on Islamic Reform movement, and I met with various groups, including an elite group from another Turkic republic. Contrasting my first night on the floor of the cell, a friend of mine gave me the key of one of his luxury apartments looking at the Bosporus Straight just above Bebek...

I was relieved the moment my airplane departed to London. When I arrived at Atlanta airport, I knew that I was at home. As much as I dislike some of the policies of the US government, especially its imperialistic and Zionist-controlled foreign policy and its promiscuous affairs with big corporations, I consider myself a very lucky person for living in a country with such a Constitution that has allowed me not to worry about expressing my progressive and liberal political and religious views. After my experience during my recent short trip, I became even more appreciative of the Constitution that protects individuals from the tyranny of government. May God reward Jefferson with eternal bliss!

Theometer or Sectometer

(First conducted on the participants of my lectures at Oxford University in November 3-5, 2008)

Edip Yuksel

Name: _____

Email Address: _____

Phone: _____ Age: _____

Occupation: _____

Nationality: _____

Have you read the Manifesto for Islamic Reform? _____

Favorite Books/Authors: _____

Your Sect: (a) Sunni (b) Shiite (c) Salafi (d) Other (d) No sect

Please put a CIRCLE around the letter of your choice:

1. According to the Quran, which one of these is not and cannot be idolized by people?
a. Prophet Muhammad
b. Desires or Wishful thinking (Hawa)
c. Crowds or peers
d. Ancestors or children
e. Reasoning (Aql)

2. Which one of these is a true statement?
a. The Quran is not sufficient to guide us; in addition we need Hadith and Sunna.
b. The Quran is not sufficient to guide us; we need Hadith, Sunna and follow the teaching of a Sunni sect.
c. The Quran is not sufficient to guide us; we need Hadith, Sunna and follow the teaching of a Shiite sect.
d. The Quran is not sufficient to guide us; we need Hadith, Sunna, follow the teaching of a sect and join a religious order.
e. The Quran is sufficient to guide us when we understand and follow it through the light of reason.

3. Which one of these hadiths narrated by Bukhari, Muslim and other "authentic" hadith books, do you think are fabricated:
a. Muhammad was illiterate until he died.
b. Muhammad married Aisha at age 54 while she was only 9 or 13 years-old.
c. Muhammad dispatched a gang of fighters (sariyya) to kill a woman poet secretly during night in her home, for criticizing him publicly through her poems.
d. Muhammad slaughtered 400 to 900 Jews belonging to Ben Qurayza for violating the treaty.
e. All of the above.

4. Which one of these laws or rules does not exist in the Quran?
a. Stone the married adulterers to death
b. Do not play guitar
c. Men should not wear silk and gold
d. Men are superior to women
e. All of the above

5. The Quran instructs us to follow the messengers. Following the messenger means:
a. Follow Hadith and Sunna; Bukhari, Muslim, Ibn Hanbal, etc.
b. Follow his Ahl-al-Bayt.
c. Follow hadith, sunna, consensus of sahaba, ijtihad of imams and fatwas of ulama.
d. Follow Muhammad.
e. Follow the message he was sent with, which was Quran alone.

6. The Quran is God's word, because:
a. There are verses of the Quran stating that it is God's word.

121

b. The Quran is a literary miracle. None can bring a sura like it surpassing its literary qualities.
c. I do not need to have a reason. Reason is not reliable. I have faith in the Quran.
d. The moral teaching of the Quran is the best for individual and humanity.
e. The Quranic signs (aya) do not have internal contradiction nor does it contradict the signs in nature. Besides, it is numerically coded book with an extraordinary mathematical structure integrated with its composition and Arabic language.

7. Which one of the following is correct for Muhammad:
a. Muhammad was the final messenger and prophet.
b. Muhammad had the highest rank above all humans.
c. Muhammad demonstrated many miracles such as splitting the moon, healing the sick, and crippling a child
d. All of the above´
e. Muhammad was a human messenger like other messengers.

8. In what year he Bukhari started collecting hadith for his hadith collection known as the Sahih Bukhari, the most trusted Sunni hadith collection?
a. During the life of Muhammad in Medina
b. Ten years after Muhammad's death.
c. 130 years after Muhammad's death.
d. 200 years after Muhammad's death
e. 230 years after Muhammad's death.

9. According to Bukhari himself, he collected the 7,275 hadith among the 700,000 hadiths he collected. If each hadith, together with its *isnad* (the chain of reporters) and *sanad* (the text that was attributed to Muhammad) took about half a book page, how many volumes of books with 500 pages would they take to record all those 700,000 hadith allegedly collected by Bukhari?
a. 7 volumes
b. 10 volumes
c. 70 volumes
d. 100 volumes
e. 700 volumes

10. What are the last statements in the Farewell Sermon (Khutba al-Wida) which was reportedly witnessed by more than 100,000 sahaba, making it by far the most authentic hadith among the thousands of hadiths?
a. I leave you Abu Bakr; you should follow him.
b. I leave you my sahaba; you may follow any of them.
c. I leave you the Quran and Sunna; you should follow both.
d. I leave you the Quran and Ahl-al-Bayt (my family); you should follow them.
e. I leave you the Quran, you should follow it.

11. According to some "authentic hadith" found in Bukhari and other hadith books, there was a verse instructing muslims to stone the married adulterers to death: "Al-shayhu wal-shayhatu iza zanaya farjumuhuma nakalan..." According to hadith reports, what happened to those verses?
a. After the Prophet Muhammad's death, Umayyad governor Marwan burned the pages where those verses were written.
b. Angle Gebrail came down and deleted it from the scripture.
c. Ibni Abbas forgot it yet Abu Hurayra never forgot it.
d. There is no reference to such a verse in any authentic hadith books.
e. After the Prophet Muhammad's death, the skin which the verse was written on was protected under Aisha's bed. A hungry goat ate it. Thus, it was abrogated literally yet kept legally.

12. According to both Bukhari and Muslim, when Muhammad was in his death bed, he asked his comrades around to bring him a paper and pen to write something for them so that they would not divert from the right path. According to the same "authentic" Sunni hadith books, Omar bin Khattab stopped a sahaba who was hurrying for a paper and pen and said the following: "The prophet is sick and has fever. He does not know what he is saying. God's book is sufficient for us." According to the hadith, all the prominent comrades (sahaba) agreed with Omar and Muhammad passed away without writing down his advice. What do you think about this hadith?

a. If it is narrated by both Bukhari and Muslim, then it must be true
b. If it is true, then, Omar and all other Sahaba must have betrayed Muhammad and committed blasphemy.
c. If it is true, then, Omar and all prominent Sahaba were followers of the Quran alone.
d. If it is false then all other hadith too should be rejected.
e. C and D must be true

13. Do we need to SAY "sallallahu alayhi wasallam" after Muhammad's name?
a. Yes, every time Muhammad is mentioned we have to praise his name.
b. Yes, but we need to say only once in our lifetime.
c. Yes, the more we say the better.
d. Yes, and those who do not say it after Muhammad's name disrespect him and they will not receive his intercession.
e. No, the Quran does not ask us to say anything after Muhammad's name; muslims were asked (salli ala) to support him, as he was also asked to support them (salli alayhim).

14. What is the correct Testimony (shahada) according to the Quran:
a. I bear witness that there is no god but the God and the Quran is God's word.
b. I bear witness that there is no god but the God and Muhammad is His messenger.
c. I bear witness that there is no god but the God and Muhammad is His messenger and His servant.
d. I bear witness that there is no god but the God and Abraham, Jesus, Moses and Muhammad are His messengers.
e. I bear witness that there is no god but the God.

15. Should Muslims who do not observe daily prayers be beaten in public?
a. Yes.
b. No.

16. Should Muslims who are caught for consuming alcohol for the fourth time be killed?
a. Yes.
b. No.

17. Did the prophet give permission to kill women and children in the war?
a. Yes.
b. No.

18. According to the Quran, are women banned from reading Quran and pray during their menstruation periods?
a. Yes
b. No.

19. In the daily Sala prayers, do you recite "attahiyyatu lillahi wassalawatu .... as salamu alayka ayyuhannabiyyu wa rahmatullahi wa barakatuhu"?
a. Yes
b. No

20. Does the Quran justify taxing Jewish and Christian population under Muslim authority with extra or different taxation called Jizya?
a. Yes
b. No.

21. Does the Quran instruct women to cover their hair?
a. Yes.
b. No.

22. Are woman restricted from leading congregational prayers?
a. Yes.
b. No.

23. Are women mentally and spiritually inferior to men?
a. Yes.
b. No.

24. Does the Quran restrict women from initiating divorce?
a. Yes.
b. No.

25. Is polygamy with previously unmarried women allowed?
a. Yes, up to four women.
b. No, polygamy is allowed only with the widows who have orphans.

26. Do pilgrims need to cast real stones at the devil?
a. Yes.
b. No.

27. Is the black stone near Kaba holy?
- a. Yes.
- b. No.

28. May a muslim own slaves?
- a. Yes.
- b. No.

29. Is circumcision a required or encouraged practice in Islam?
- a. Yes.
- b. No.

30. Should converts change their names to Arabic names?
- a. Yes.
- b. No.

31. How much *zaka* charity one should give away?
- a. 2.5%
- b. As much as one can afford, without making themselves needy.

32. Are those who break their fast during Ramadan before the sunset required to fast 60 consecutive days as a punishment for not completing the day?
- a. Yes.
- b. No.

33. Is leadership the right of Quraish tribe?
- a. Yes.
- b. No.

34. Is drawing pictures or making three dimensional statutes a sin?
- a. Yes.
- b. No.

35. Are there more dietary prohibitions besides pork, carcass, running blood, and animal dedicated to idolized names?
- a. Yes.
- b. No.

36. Is displaying Muhammad's name and the names of his closest companions next to God's name in the mosques idol-worship?
- a. Yes.
- b. No.

37. Did Muhammad advise some sick people to drink camel urine?
- a. Yes.
- b. No.

38. Did Muhammad gauge people's eyes with hot nails?
- a. Yes.
- b. No.

39. After following the advice of Moses, did Muhammad, bargain with God about the number of prayers, lowering down from the impossible-to-observe 50 times a day to 5 times a day?
- a. Yes.
- b. No.

40. Does Muhammad have the power of intercession?
- a. Yes.
- b. No.

41. Was Muhammad sinless?
- a. Yes.
- b. No.

42. Did God create the universe for the sake of Muhammad?
- a. Yes.
- b. No.

43. Did Muhammad have sexual power of 30 males?
- a. Yes.
- b. No.

44. Was Muhammad bewitched by a Jew?
- a. Yes.
- b. No.

45. Do some verses of the Quran abrogate other verses?
- a. Yes.
- b. No.

Here is the story and the answer of this test:

Between November 3 and 10 of 2008, I traveled to UK and Turkey to deliver four lectures; first two at Oxford University, the third at Muslim Institute in London and the fourth one in Istanbul Book Fair. I had prepared a test containing 45 multiple choice questions just the night before my travel. I duplicated them on both sides of a single sheet and I distributed to the audience before the lecture... They were asked to write their name, age, occupation, email address, favorite authors, and their sectarian affiliation. It was a bit awkward to test an audience that consisted of students and professors at one of the world's top universities. The multiple-choice test proved to be a powerful instrument to deliver the message of Islamic Reform under the light of the Quran. The correct answer for each multiple choice question was the E option, and for the Yes or No questions was the B option. So, it would take me a few seconds to evaluate the tests after they were returned to me.

The Sunni or Shiite test-takers found themselves in quagmire of contradiction with their own sectarian teachings. They learned that they were thirty, forty or even more than fifty percent infidels or heretics. Some of those who marked Sunni as their sectarian affiliation contradicted the Sunni teachings on most of the issues. According to their own confessed sects, their lives were worthless; they deserved to be killed! I did not let this mirror or sect-o-meter remain an individual experience; I publicly declared the overall results. Many got all answers correct, including Eric, a monotheist from Unitarian church who already had a copy of the Quran: a Reformist Translation in his possession. Eric knew the original message of islam better than all the mullahs and the so-called "ulama" combined.

If you have chosen the wrong option for any of the questions and you are wondering why you have contradicted the Quran, please visit **www.islamicreform.org** and read the full version of the Manifesto for Islamic Reform. If you prefer to have it in a book form, you may order it by visiting **www.brainbowpress.com**

Brainbow Press Publications

Quran: A Reformist Translation
Translated and Annotated by: Edip Yuksel; Layth Saleh al-Shaiban; Martha Schulte-Nafeh. Brainbow Press, 2007, 520 pages, $24.70. ISBN 978-0-9796715-0-0

Test Your Quranic Knowledge
Contains six sets of multiple choice questions and their answers. Edip Yuksel, Brainbow Press, 2007, 52 pages, $7.95. ISBN 978-0-9796715-5-5

Manifesto for Islamic Reform
Edip Yuksel, Brainbow Press, 2008, 88 pages, $9.95. ISBN 978-0-9796715-6-2

The Natural Republic
Layth Saleh al-Shaiban (ProgressiveMuslims.org), Brainbow Press, 2008, 198 pages, $14.95. ISBN 978-0-9796715-8-6

Critical Thinkers for Islamic Reform
A Collection of Articles from Contemporary Thinkers on Islam Editors: Edip Yuksel, Arnold Y Mol, Farouk A. Peru, Brainbow Press, 2009, 260 pages, $17.00. ISBN 978-0-9796715-7-9

Edip Yuksel's Upcoming Books in years 2009-2011

- **In the Name of Allah: My Journey from Radicalism to Reform**
  An autobiography.
- **NINETEEN: God's Signature in Nature and Scripture**
  A comprehensive demonstration of the prophetic miracle.
- **Running Like Zebras**
  Edip Yüksel's debate with the critics of Code 19
- **19 Questions for Muslims, Christians, and Atheists**
  The first two sections are revisions of old booklets.
- **Purple Letters**
  A selection of correspondence on religion, philosophy, and politics.
- **From Faith to Reason: Inspiring Stories of Forty Monotheists**
  Inspiring stories of forty converts from Sunni, Shiite, Catholic, Protestant religions and Atheism to Islam.
- **The Bestest Teacher, Student and Parent:**
  57 Rules for Students, Teachers and Parents.
- **Twelve Hungry Men**
  A religious/political/philosophical comedy for a feature film
- **The American Janus**
  A political mirror and x-ray of America's best and worst.
- **Muhammad: A Messenger of Peace and Reason**
  A script for an animated feature film about Muhammad's mission.

Join the Movement; Let the World Know!

The Islamic Reform movement is receiving momentum around the globe. We invite you to join us in our activities locally, internationally. Please contact us through the contact addresses posted at:

www.islamicreform.org
www.free-minds.org
www.mpjp.org
www.19.org

To study the Quran more diligently, you may visit 19.org for links to computer programs, searchable Quranic indexes, electronic versions of this and other translations, and various study tools. We highly recommend you the following sites for your study of the Quran:

www.quranix.com
www.openquran.org
www.studyquran.org
www.quranmiracles.org

****

www.19.org
www.yuksel.org
www.free-minds.org
www.islamicreform.org
www.quranmiracles.org
www.brainbowpress.com
www.groups.google.com/group/19org
www.deenresearchcenter.com
www.quranbrowser.com
www.openburhan.com
www.studyquran.org
www.quranix.com
www.mpjp.org

…and more